COMPANION

FIESTA

Mark F. Moran
Glen Victorey

©2006 Krause Publications

Published by

krause publications
An Imprint of F+W Publications

700 East State Street • Iola, WI 54990-0001
715-445-2214 • 888-457-2873

Our toll-free number to place an order or obtain
a free catalog is (800) 258-0929.

Library of Congress Catalog Number: 2006922212
ISBN 13-digit: 978-0-89689-431-0
ISBN 10-digit: 0-89689-431-2

Designed by Donna Mummery
Edited by Mary Sieber

Printed in China

Table of Contents

On the Road to Fiesta   4
Fiesta Colors   5
The Red Scare   6
Dimensions and Colors   6
Bottom Marks   7

Vintage Fiesta Pieces   9
Ashtrays   10
Bowls   13
    Covered onion soup bowl   13
    Cream soup cup   17
    Dessert bowl   19
    Footed salad bowl   23
    4-3/4" fruit bowl   26
    5-1/2" fruit bowl   32
    11-3/4" fruit bowl   38
    Individual salad bowl   40
    Mixing bowl #1   42
    Mixing bowl #2   45
    Mixing bowl #3   47
    Mixing bowl #4   49
    Mixing bowl #5   51
    Mixing bowl #6   52
    Mixing bowl #7   54
    Mixing bowl lids   56
    8-1/2" nappy   58
    9-1/2" nappy   62
Candleholders   63
    Bulb candleholder   63
    Tripod candleholder   65
Carafes   67
Casseroles   71
Coffeepots   75
    Demitasse coffeepot   76
Comports   79
    Sweets comport   80
Creamers & sugar bowls   81
    Ring-handle creamer   81
    Stick-handle creamer   83
    Sugar bowl   84
Cups & mugs   86
    Demitasse cup and saucer   86
    Eggcup   88
    Teacup and saucer   90
    Tom & Jerry mug   93
Marmalade jar   96
Mustard jar   98

Pitchers & jugs   100
    Disk water pitcher   100
    Ice pitcher   105
    Syrup pitcher   107
    Two-pint jug   109
Plates   112
    6" plate   112
    7" plate   114
    9" plate   117
    10" plate   126
    Cake plate   130
    Calendar plate   132
    13" chop plate   133
    15" chop plate   136
    10-1/2" compartment plate   138
    12" compartment plate   140
    Deep plate   142
Platters   146
Salt and pepper shakers   150
Sauceboats   155
Teapots   160
    Medium teapot   160
    Large teapot   163
Trays   164
    Relish tray   164
    Tidbit tray   167
    Utility tray   168
Tumblers   170
    Water tumbler   170
Vases   172
    Bud vase   172
    8" vase   175
    10" vase   177
    12" vase   179
Promotional Items   180
    Unlisted salad bowl   181
    Casserole with pie plate   184
    French casserole   185
    Creamer/sugar and tray set   187
    Disk juice pitcher   189
    Juice tumbler   190
Post '86 Fiesta   193
Amberstone, Casuals, Casualstone,
    Ironstone   233
Striped Fiesta   244
Fiesta Kitchen Kraft   246
Commemoratives   257
Fiesta Go-Alongs   267

On the Road to Fiesta

The Homer Laughlin China Company originated with a two-kiln pottery on the banks of the Ohio River in East Liverpool, Ohio. Built in 1873-'74 by Homer Laughlin and his brother, Shakespeare, the firm was first known as the Ohio Valley Pottery, and later Laughlin Bros. Pottery. It was one of the first white-ware plants in the country.

After a tentative beginning, the company was awarded a prize for having the best white-ware at the 1876 Centennial Exposition in Philadelphia.

Under new ownership in 1907, the headquarters and a new 30-kiln plant were built across the Ohio River in Newell, West Virginia, the present manufacturing and headquarters location.

In the 1920s, two additions to the Homer Laughlin staff set the stage for the company's greatest success: the Fiesta line.

Dr. Albert V. Bleininger was hired in 1920. A scientist, author, and educator, he oversaw the conversion from bottle kilns to the more efficient tunnel kilns.

In 1927, the company hired designer Frederick Hurten Rhead. A member of a distinguished family of English ceramists, Rhead began to develop the artistic quality of the company's wares, and to experiment with shapes and glazes. In 1935, this work culminated in his designs for the Fiesta line.

Fiesta Colors

Fiesta wares were produced in 14 colors (other than special promotions) from 1936 to 1972. These are usually divided into the "original colors" of cobalt blue, light green, ivory, red, turquoise, and yellow (cobalt blue, green, red, and yellow only on the Kitchen Kraft line, introduced in 1939); the "Fifties colors" of chartreuse, forest green, gray, rose, and medium green; plus the later additions of Casuals, Amberstone, Fiesta Ironstone, and Casualstone ("Coventry") in antique gold, mango red, and turf green; and the Striped, Decal, and Lustre pieces. No Fiesta was produced from 1973 to 1985. The colors that make up the "original" and "Fifties" groups along with medium green are sometimes referred to as "the standard eleven."

In many pieces, medium green is the hardest to find and most expensive Fiesta color.

Fiesta colors and years of production up to 1972

Cobalt Blue—dark or "royal" blue (1936-1951)

Ivory—creamy, slightly yellowed (1936-1951)

Green—often called Light Green when comparing it to other green glazes, also called "original" green (1936-1951)

Red—reddish orange (1936-1944 and 1959-1972)

Yellow—golden yellow (1936-1969)

Turquoise—sky blue, like the stone (1937-1969)

Chartreuse—yellowish green (1951-1959)

Forest Green—dark "hunter" green (1951-1959)

Gray—light or ash gray (1951-1959)

Rose—dusty, dark rose (1951-1959)

Medium Green—bright rich green (1959-1969)

Antique Gold—dark butterscotch (1969-1972)

Turf Green—olive (1969-1972)

Mango Red—same as original red (1970-1972)

The Red Scare

During World War II, the U.S. government restricted the use of uranium oxide, which gave Fiesta red its color. This restriction was not lifted until 1959. Though the company then used a different formulation for the red glaze, people were still concerned about vintage glazes with even a minute uranium or heavy metal content. The Food and Drug Administration had previously determined that daily use of vintage dinnerware as serving pieces does not pose a hazard, as long as the glazes and decals were properly applied. To be on the safe side, avoid storing food in any vintage pieces, and do not use them in a microwave oven.

Dimensions and Colors

Even though we have provided detailed dimensions for each Fiesta piece, the nature of the machinery used to make each item, and the skill of the potters who applied some details by hand, result in variations throughout the line.

Some glazes also have several shades, to the point that even seasoned collectors and antique dealers may mistake an especially heavy light green glaze for the more rare medium green. Some glazes are also prone to mottling, including turquoise and—to a lesser degree—red. Cobalt blue and turf green pieces tend to show even the slightest scratches more obviously than lighter glazes, and Ivory examples often exhibit cloudy or sooty spots along rims and bases.

And remember that Fiesta colors will also look different depending on the light at hand. Incandescent, fluorescent, and natural light will each add a different color element.

Editor's Note: Every effort was made to ensure that the photographs in this book present the Fiesta line in its proper colors. Slight differences in the color of the glazes used when the Fiesta items were produced, as well as the quality of some of the images, may distort the color of some pieces pictured in this book.

Bottom Marks

Bottom of 6" bread plates in green, turquoise, and yellow, showing "Genuine Fiesta" stamp and three marks left during firing by the sagger pins.

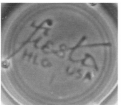  

Bottom of No. 1 mixing bowl in green, showing sagger pin marks, the "Fiesta/HLCo. USA" impressed mark, and the faint "1" size indicator. The impressed size mark on the bottom of the No. 2 mixing bowl in yellow is too faint to be seen in this image.

Bottom of a teacup saucer in turquoise, showing sagger pin marks and the "Genuine Fiesta" stamp. Note the difference in the ring pattern when compared to the turquoise bread plate.

Examples of impressed Fiesta bottom marks.

An ink stamp on the bottom of a piece of Fiesta.

Two different impressed marks on the bottoms of relish tray inserts.

Notice the different bottoms of two ashtrays. The top one has a set of rings with no room for a logo. The lower ashtray has rings along the outer edge, opposite of the ring pattern on the ashtray above.

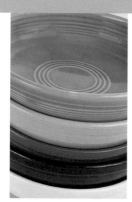

VINTAGE FIESTA PIECES

Ashtrays

Dimensions: 6-1/4" by 1-1/4"
Production Dates: 1936 through 1969
There are two bottom variations known. Before 1940, the base has seven rings and is not marked; after 1940, the base has two rings and a "Genuine Fiesta" stamp. Production of red examples was halted in 1944 and resumed in 1959.

Degree of Difficulty: 1 for all colors other than Medium Green, which ranks 3.

Chartreuse	**$69-$79**	Gray	**$70-$76**	Red	**$56-$65**
Cobalt Blue	**$50-$59**	Ivory	**$50-$59**	Rose	**$72-$80**
Forest Green	**$74-$85**	Medium Green		Turquoise	**$44-$56**
Light Green	**$49-$54**		**$185-$206**	Yellow	**$39-$45**

Stack of four ashtrays in yellow, cobalt blue, ivory, and red.

Ashtray in red. **$56-$65**

Ashtray in cobalt blue.
$50-$59

Ashtray in ivory. **$50-$59**

Ashtray in yellow. **$39-$45**

Four ashtrays in yellow, red, ivory, and cobalt blue.

Stack of four ashtrays in red, cobalt blue, ivory and yellow.

Ashtray in light green.
$49-$54

Ashtray in light green. **$49-$54**

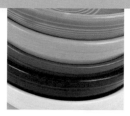

Bowls

Covered onion soup bowl

Dimensions: 6-1/8" by 4-1/2" by 4-3/8" tall with lid

Production Dates: 1936 to late 1937

Because of the short period of time covered onion soup bowls were produced, they are hard to find. Expect to pay a premium price for a rare turquoise example because the bowls were discontinued at about the same time that the turquoise glaze was introduced.

Degree of Difficulty: 3 for colors other than turquoise, which ranks 5+.

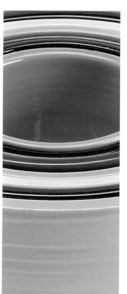

Cobalt Blue	$660-$729
Ivory	$660-$729
Light Green	$600-$658
Red	$645-$725
Yellow	$580-$650
Turquoise	$6,593-$7,656

Covered onion soup bowl in ivory. **$660-$729**

Covered onion soup bowl in light green. **$600-$658**

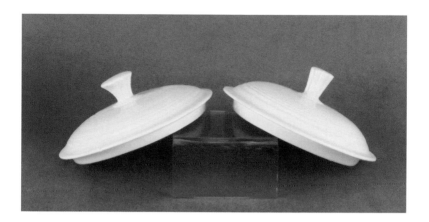

Two covered onion soup bowls and lids in ivory. The lid on the left is the typical production style with a more flared knob and shorter flange ring; the lid on the right is the early production style and has a more tapered knob and deeper flange ring. The more common one on the left is valued at **$660-$729.** There is no established value for the one on the right.

Covered onion soup bowl in yellow. **$580-$650**

Covered onion soup bowl in cobalt blue. **$660-$729**

Cream soup cup

Dimensions: 6-5/8" by 5-1/16" by 2-1/4" tall
Production Dates: 1936 until 1959
The wide C-shaped or "lug" handle is unique because this was the only Fiesta piece that had this handle. Because the handles were added by hand, you may come across a cream soup cup with crooked handles, or handles that are not exactly across from each other. Bottom marks vary, but all have four rings. Production of red examples was halted in 1944 and resumed in 1959.

Degree of Difficulty: 1-2 for colors other than medium green, which ranks 5+.

Chartreuse	$62-$70	Red	$58-$70
Cobalt Blue	$54-$65	Rose	$62-$73
Forest Green	$65-$74	Turquoise	$43-$49
Gray	$61-$72	Yellow	$41-$47
Ivory	$52-$62	Medium Green	$4,426-$4,757
Light Green	$44-$50		

Cream soup cup in turquoise.
$43-$49

Cream soup cup in gray.
$61-$72

Cream soup cups in ivory, **$52-$62,** turquoise, **$43-$49**, and red, **$58-$70**.

Dessert bowl

Dimensions: 6-1/4" by 1-1/4"
Production Dates: 1936 until late 1960
Examples can be found with either four or five interior rings. Production of red examples was halted in 1944 and resumed in 1959.

Degree of Difficulty: 1 for the original six colors; 2 for the 1950s colors; and 4-5 for medium green.

Chartreuse	$46-$51	Red	$42-$52
Cobalt Blue	$40-$50	Rose	$50-$56
Forest Green	$46-$51	Turquoise	$35-$45
Gray	$49-$54	Yellow	$34-$45
Ivory	$41-$50	Medium Green	$640-$695
Light Green	$36-$46		

Dessert bowl in medium green. **$640-$695**

Dessert bowls in six original colors.

Dessert bowl in yellow.
$34-$45

Dessert bowl in rose.
$50-$56

Dessert bowl in ivory.
$41-$50

Dessert bowl in chartreuse.
$46-$51

Dessert bowl in forest
green. **$46-$51**

Dessert bowl in gray.
$49-$54

Dessert bowls in cobalt blue, **$40-$50,** red, **$42-$52**, and turquoise, **$35-$45**.

Dessert bowl in red. **$42-$52**

Dessert bowl in turquoise. **$35-$45**

Dessert bowl in cobalt blue. **$40-$50**

Dessert bowls in turquoise, **$35-$45,** light green, **$36-$46**, and red, **$42-$52**.

Footed salad bowl

Dimensions: 11-3/8" by 5-1/2"
Production Dates: 1936 to 1946

One of the original items in the line when it debuted in January 1936, this bowl was also used as the punch bowl in the Tom & Jerry set Variations on this bowl include the foot that was applied by different techniques, leaving it either thick or thin, and two different back stamps, either ink stamped or in-mold. Production of red examples was halted in 1944.

Degree of Difficulty: 3-4

Cobalt Blue	**$410-$460**	Red	**$415-$475**
Ivory	**$385-$445**	Turquoise	**$387-$399**
Light Green	**$387-$395**	Yellow	**$375-$395**

Footed salad bowl in red. **$415-$475**

Footed salad bowl in ivory. **$385-$445**

Footed salad bowl in yellow. **$375-$395**

Footed salad bowl in cobalt blue. **$410-$460**

4-3/4" Fruit bowl

Dimensions: 4-3/4" by 1-1/2"
Production Dates: 1938 to mid-1959
Due to its long production run, there are several variations in the number of rings inside the bowl as well as the size of the rings. The other variation (except in medium green) is on the underside of this piece. Early examples were completely glazed so you will find sagger pin marks—three equally spaced on the bottom. Later bowls have a wiped foot. Production of red was halted in 1944 and resumed in 1959.

Degree of Difficulty: 1-2 for colors other than medium green, which ranks 4-5.

4-3/4" fruit bowl in medium green. **$600-$650**

Chartreuse	$32-$36
Cobalt Blue	$27-$32
Forest Green	$33-$37
Gray	$30-$35
Light Green	$25-$30
Ivory	$28-$32
Red	$31-$33
Rose	$30-$37
Turquoise	$23-$29
Yellow	$23-$27
Medium Green	$600-$650

Two light green fruit bowls, one 4-3/4" and the other 5-1/2", showing the variation in color intensity and ring patterns.

4-3/4" fruit bowls in chartreuse, **$32-$36,** forest green, **$33-$37**, turquoise, **$23-$29**, ivory, **$28-$32**, and yellow, **$23-$27**.

4-3/4" fruit bowl in light green. **$25-$30**

4-3/4" fruit bowl in turquoise. **$23-$29**

4-3/4" fruit bowl in cobalt blue. **$27-$32**

4-3/4" fruit bowl in red. **$31-$33**

4-3/4" fruit bowl in ivory. **$28-$32**

4-3/4" fruit bowl in yellow. **$23-$27**

Fruit bowls in turquoise, **$23-$29,** cobalt blue, **$27-$32,** red, **$31-$33,** ivory, **$28-$32,** yellow, **$23-$27,** and light green, **$25-$30**.

5-1/2" Fruit bowl

Dimensions: 5-1/2" by 1-3/4"
Production Dates: 1936 to late 1969
Both this bowl and the 4-3/4" fruit bowl are scaled-down versions of the 8-1/2" and 9-1/2" nappies. The variations on this bowl are the same as the ones on its smaller sibling, the 4-3/4" fruit bowl. Production of red examples was halted in 1944 and resumed 1959.

Degree of Difficulty: 1 for the original colors; 2 for the 1950s colors; and 3 for medium green.

5-1/2" fruit bowl in medium green. **$67-$72**

Chartreuse	$32-$39
Cobalt Blue	$26-$35
Forest Green	$32-$40
Gray	$32-$38
Light Green	$24-$31
Ivory	$27-$34
Red	$27-$35
Rose	$33-$39
Turquoise	$23-$30
Yellow	$23-$30
Medium Green	$67-$72

5-1/2" fruit bowl in gray. **$32-$38**

5-1/2" fruit bowl in red.
$27-$35

5-1/2" fruit bowl in chartreuse. **$32-$39**

5-1/2" fruit bowl in rose. **$33-$39**

5-1/2" fruit bowl in ivory. **$27-$34**

5-1/2" fruit bowl in cobalt blue. **$26-$35**

5-1/2" fruit bowl in turquoise. **$23-$30**

5-1/2" fruit bowl in yellow. **$23-$30**

5-1/2" fruit bowl in forest green. **$32-$40**

5-1/2" fruit bowl in light green, **$24-$31.**

5-1/2" fruit bowls in turquoise, **$23-$30,** ivory, **$27-$34,** and light green, **$24-$31**.

11-3/4 in. Fruit bowl

Dimensions: 11-3/8" by 3"
Production Dates: 1937 to 1946
This bowl was designed by Frederick Rhead to be part of the Kitchen Kraft line. When the bowl was not approved by Homer Laughlin Co. management for the Kitchen Kraft line, it was added to the Fiesta line. You will notice the lack of rings under the flange (lip) of the bowl. Production of red examples was halted in 1944.

Degree of Difficulty: 3-4

Cobalt Blue	$295-$340	Red	$310-$340
Ivory	$295-$330	Turquoise	$285-$335
Light Green	$280-$320	Yellow	$280-$315

11-3/4" fruit bowl in red, with factory flaw. **$310-$340**

11-3/4" fruit bowl in ivory. **$295-$330**

11-3/4" fruit bowl in light green. **$280-$320**

11-3/4" fruit bowl in yellow. **$280-$315**

Individual salad bowl

Dimensions: 7-5/8" by 2-3/8"
Production Dates: 1959-1969

The individual salad bowl made its Fiesta debut in 1959, the first new item in the line since 1940. Although Homer Laughlin Co.'s Harlequin line offered a very similar bowl in its line in 1939, it would take 20 years for the company to add it to Fiesta. Although the individual salad bowl was produced for approximately 10 years, it is slightly harder to find than other Fiesta bowls. Marks include the impressed "Fiesta/Made in USA" or the "Genuine Fiesta" stamp.

Degree of Difficulty: 2-3

Red	$90-$105	Yellow	$80-$90
Turquoise	$85-$90	Medium Green	$110-$120

Individual salad bowl in red. **$90-$105**

Individual salad bowl in turquoise.
$85-$90

Individual salad bowl in medium green.
$110-$120

Individual salad bowl in yellow. **$80-$90**

Mixing bowl #1

Dimensions: 3-1/2" by 5"
Production Dates: 1937 to 1946
Production of these bowls lasted approximately 8-1/2 years. Late in 1942 the #1 mixing bowl was available only in red. Bowls made before 1938 have rings inside the bottom, and are usually marked "Fiesta/HLC USA" and the size number. Bowls made later have no rings and are usually marked "Fiesta/Made in USA" and the size number. Part of the selling point of these bowls was that the customer could purchase whichever size bowl was needed. The smallest (#1) and the largest (#7) must not have sold well, as they are hardest to find today.

Degree of Difficulty: 3-4

| Cobalt Blue | $215-$248 | Light Green | $190-$215 | Turquoise | $225-$250 |
| Ivory | $215-$245 | Red | $200-$235 | Yellow | $195-$210 |

Nested mixing bowls.

No. 1 mixing bowl in red, **$200-$235,** with an ivory lid, **$875-$1,000**.

No. 1 mixing
bowl in turquoise.
$225-$250.

Mixing bowl #2

Dimensions: 4" by 5-7/8"
Production Dates: 1937 to 1946
Late in 1942 this size was available only in yellow. Bowls made before 1938 have rings inside the bottom, and are usually marked "Fiesta/HLC USA." Bowls made later have no rings and are usually marked "Fiesta/Made in USA." Although all seven bowls were originally offered in all six Fiesta colors, after mid-1942, each bowl was only offered in one color.

Degree of Difficulty: 2

| Cobalt Blue | $118-$147 | Light Green | $112-$140 | Turquoise | $118-$143 |
| Ivory | $127-$156 | Red | $120-$149 | Yellow | $115-$140 |

No. 2 mixing bowl in turquoise, **$118-$143,** with a cobalt blue lid, **$900-$1,100.**

No. 2 mixing bowl in cobalt blue. **$118-$147**

No. 2 mixing bowl in yellow. **$115-$140**

Mixing bowl #3

Dimensions: 4-1/2" by 6-3/4"
Production Dates: 1937 to 1946
Late in 1942 this size was available only in light green. Bowls made before 1938 have rings inside the bottom, and are usually marked "Fiesta/HLC USA." Bowls made later have no rings and are usually marked "Fiesta/Made in USA." Originally, all seven mixing bowls had rings inside the bottom. During the course of the production run, the bowls lost the inside rings—no doubt making it easier to mix and to clean the bowls.

Degree of Difficulty: 2

Cobalt Blue	$138-$165	Light Green	$122-$145	Turquoise	$130-$155
Ivory	$137-$160	Red	$135-$158	Yellow	$125-$150

No. 3 mixing bowl, **$125-$150,** and lid in yellow, **$800-$900.**

No. 3 mixing bowl in cobalt blue, **$138-$165,** and lid in cobalt blue, **$900-$1,100.**

No. 3 mixing bowl in red. **$135-$158**

Mixing bowl #4

Dimensions: 5" by 7-3/4"
Production Dates: 1937 to 1946

Late in 1942 this size was available only in ivory. Bowls made before 1938 have rings inside the bottom, and are usually marked "Fiesta/HLC USA" and the size number. Bowls made later have no rings and are usually marked "Fiesta/Made in USA" and the size number. After approximately five years, the mixing bowls were only available in one color each. Starting with the smallest size (#1), the colors chosen were:

#1	Red		#5	Yellow
#2	Yellow		#6	Turquoise
#3	Light Green		#7	Cobalt Blue
#4	Ivory			

Degree of Difficulty: 2

Cobalt Blue	**$145-$173**	Ivory	**$152-$178**	Turquoise	**$130-$157**
Light Green	**$127-$153**	Red	**$142-$170**	Yellow	**$121-$148**

No. 4 mixing bowl in cobalt blue. **$145-$173**

No. 4 mixing bowl in ivory. **$152-$178**

No. 4 mixing bowl in turquoise. **$130-$157**

Mixing bowl #5

Dimensions: 5-3/4" by 8-1/2"
Production Dates: 1937 to 1946
Late in 1942 this size was available only in yellow. Bowls made before 1938 have rings inside the bottom, and are usually marked "Fiesta/HLC USA" and the size number. Bowls made later have no rings and are usually marked "Fiesta/Made in USA" and the size number. The set of seven bowls as also known as nesting bowls because they fit (or nested) inside each other. A housewife of the Depression era could store a set of seven bowls in the space it took to store the largest bowl.

Degree of Difficulty: 2

Cobalt Blue	$205-$238	Light Green	$174-$194	Turquoise	$190-$199
Ivory	$200-$237	Red	$202-$225	Yellow	$170-$185

No. 5 mixing bowl in ivory.
$200-$237

Mixing bowl #6

Dimensions: 6-1/4" by 9-3/4"
Production Dates: 1937 to 1946
Late in 1942 this size was available only in turquoise. Bowls made before 1938 have rings inside the bottom, and are usually marked "Fiesta/HLC USA" and the size number. Bowls made later have no rings and are usually marked "Fiesta/Made in USA" and the size number.

Degree of Difficulty: 3

Cobalt Blue	**$285-$332**	Red	**$282-$327**
Ivory	**$280-$327**	Turquoise	**$270-$317**
Light Green	**$249-$299**	Yellow	**$253-$299**

No. 6 mixing bowl in red. **$282-$327**

No. 6 mixing bowl in cobalt blue. **$285-$332**

Mixing bowl #7

Dimensions: 7-1/8" by 11"
Production Dates: 1936 to 1944
Late in 1942 this size was available only in cobalt blue. Bowls made before 1938 have rings inside the bottom, and are usually marked "Fiesta/HLC USA" and the size number. Bowls made later have no rings and are usually marked with "Fiesta/Made in USA" and the size number. There are no known lids for this size bowl.

The #7 mixing bowl holds the distinction of being the heaviest (6-1/2 pounds) item in the entire Fiesta line.

Degree of Difficulty: 3-4

Cobalt Blue	$399-$489	Ivory	$448-$489	Turquoise	$395-$425
Light Green	$370-$435	Red	$423-$475	Yellow	$370-$425

No. 7 mixing bowl in ivory.
$448-$489

No. 7 mixing bowl in cobalt blue.
$399-$489

No. 7 mixing bowl in yellow. **$370-$425**

Mixing Bowl Lids

Dimensions: #1, 5"; #2, 6"; #3, 6-3/4"; #4, 7-3/4"
Production Dates: for approximately six months in late 1936.
Although lids for all seven mixing bowls were modeled, only the four smallest ones were ever put into production. Having been produced for less than half a year, lids are some of the hardest to find items in the regular Fiesta line. If you ever have the chance to purchase a #5 or #6 lid, expect to pay $10,000 or more. Although there are rumors of a #7 lid having survived, so far none has surfaced. Lids have been found in the first five colors. No turquoise lid has ever been found.

Degree of Difficulty: 5

Cobalt Blue	$900-$1,100	Light Green	$800-$900	Yellow	$800-$900
Ivory	$875-$1,000	Red	$900-$1,100		

No. 3 mixing bowl in red, **$135-$158,** with lid in light green, **$800-$900.**
Lid in red, **$900-$1,100;** lid in yellow, **$800-$900.**

Very rare bowl lids in red, **$900-$1,100,** yellow, **$800-$900,** and light green, **$800-$900**.

8-1/2" Nappy

Dimensions: 8-1/2" by 2-7/8"
Production Dates: 1936 to 1969

Nappy is a British term for a shallow, rimless serving bowl. Although "nappy" is not a common term today, the name was much more common when Fiesta made its debut in 1936. A serving bowl has been a standard piece in dinnerware forever—and a popular item in the Fiesta line, so much so that a slightly larger version was also made. Impressed marks include "Fiesta/HLC USA" before 1938, and "Fiesta/Made in USA" after 1938. Production of red examples was halted in 1944 and resumed in 1959.

Degree of Difficulty: 1 for the original six colors, 2 for colors of the 1950s, and 3 for medium green.

Chartreuse	**$65-$67**
Cobalt Blue	**$53-$58**
Forest Green	**$60-$63**
Gray	**$59-$61**
Ivory	**$50-$57**
Light Green	**$44-$47**
Red	**$55-$60**
Rose	**$59-$62**
Turquoise	**$45-$46**
Yellow	**$45-$49**
Medium Green	
	$170-$185

8-1/2" nappy in medium green. **$170-$185**

8-1/2" nappy in light green.
$44-$47

8-1/2" nappy in ivory,
with faint spots of sooty
discoloration around the rim
typical of pieces in this color.
$50-$57

8-1/2" nappy in cobalt blue.
$53-$58

8-1/2" nappy in turquoise.
$45-$46

8-1/2" nappy in red. **$55-$60**

8-1/2" nappy in rose. **$59-$62**

8-1/2" nappy in chartreuse.
$65-$67

8-1/2" nappy in yellow.
$45-$49

9-1/2" Nappy

Dimensions: 9-1/2" by 3-1/8"
Production Dates: 1936 to 1947
Although the 9-1/2" nappy was produced for only 11 years (one-third the length of time the 8-1/2" nappy was produced), examples are still relatively easy to find. Prices for this piece are reasonable and not much more than its sibling, the 8-1/2" nappy. Impressed marks include "Fiesta/HLC USA" (two sizes) before 1938, and "Fiesta/Made in USA" after 1938. Production of red examples was halted in 1944.

Degree of Difficulty: 1-2

Cobalt Blue	**$70-$75**	Light Green	**$55-$59**	Turquoise	**$56-$59**
Ivory	**$69-$71**	Red	**$75-$81**	Yellow	**$57-$60**

9-1/2" nappy in ivory. **$69-$71**

9-1/2" nappy in red. **$75-$81**

Candleholders

Bulb candleholders

Dimensions: 3-3/4" by 2-1/2"
Production Dates: 1936 to 1946

These candleholders are pure art deco. Housewives of the 1930s must have loved the bulb candleholders more than the tripod variety, as many of them seem to have been purchased. This is a great example of how the Fiesta line was promoted as not only suitable for breakfast and lunch, but for dinner and parties, too. Red was discontinued in 1944. They are marked inside the base "Fiesta HLCo USA."

Degree of Difficulty: 2

Cobalt Blue	$115-$125/pair
Ivory	$115-$125/pair
Light Green	$95-$115/pair
Red	$120-$130/pair
Turquoise	$115-$125/pair
Yellow	$105-$110/pair

Bulb candleholder in cobalt blue.
$115-$125/pair

Bulb candleholder in ivory.
$115-$125/pair

Bulb candleholder in yellow.
$105-$110/pair

Tripod candleholders

Dimensions: 3-1/2" by 4-1/2"
Production Dates: 1936 to 1943
The tripod candleholders are one of the most sought-after items in the vintage Fiesta line. If you are lucky enough to find a pair, check the three "supports" for chips and flaking. They are also part of the post-'86 wares. The early versions are marked with an impressed "Fiesta/HLC USA.." One way to tell a vintage holder from a new one (other than the color range) is that almost all early holders have a completely glazed base, called a "wet foot." New holders have the glaze wiped from the base.

Degree of Difficulty: 4

Cobalt Blue	**$575-$630/pair**	Red	**$625-$660/pair**
Ivory	**$600-$650/pair**	Turquoise	**$625-$685/pair**
Light Green	**$500-$550/pair**	Yellow	**$500-$525/pair**

Bulb candleholders in red, **$120-$130/pair,** and tripod candleholders in light green, **$500-$550/pair.**

Tripod candleholders in yellow, **$500-$525/pair,** light green, **$500-$550/pair**, and ivory, **$600-$650/pair**.

Tripod candleholders in cobalt blue, **$575-$630/pair,** and red, **$625-$660/pair**.

Carafes

Dimensions: 9-1/4" by 7-1/8" by 6-1/8"
Production Dates: 1936 to 1947

Along with the disk pitcher, the carafe is one of the most photographed pieces of the entire Fiesta line —perhaps because its style represents art deco in its purist form. The stopper has a cork attached. Before buying, check the cork for deterioration and damage. The carafe holds 6-1/2 cups. Red was discontinued in 1944. It is marked with an impressed "Fiesta/HLC USA."

Degree of Difficulty: 2-3

Cobalt Blue	**$300-$345**
Ivory	**$310-$320**
Light Green	**$275-$295**
Red	**$295-$335**
Turquoise	**$265-$300**
Yellow	**$250-$285**

Carafe in turquoise.
$265-$300

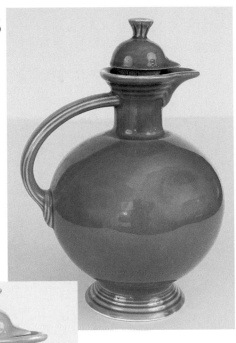

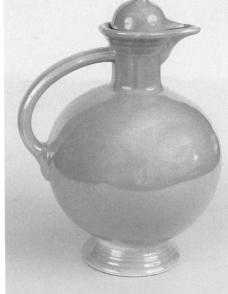

Carafe in yellow.
$250-$285

Carafe in cobalt blue.
$300-$345

Carafe in light green.
$275-$295

Carafes in red, **$295-$335,** and ivory, **$310-$320**.

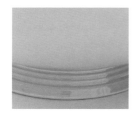

Casseroles

Covered casserole

Dimensions: 9-3/4" by 7-7/8" by 5-3/4" tall with lid

Production Dates: 1936 to 1969

In styling, the covered casserole is a larger version of the covered onion soup bowl, and a shirt-tale relative of the sugar bowl. A covered dish has been a standard piece in almost all dinnerware sets, regardless of the country of origin. The casserole has two impressed marks: "Fiesta/HLC USA" and the later "Fiesta/Made in USA." Production of red examples was halted in 1944 and resumed in 1959.

Degree of Difficulty: 2 for the original colors; 3 for the colors of the 1950s and medium green.

Chartreuse	**$250-$260**
Cobalt Blue	**$195-$215**
Forest Green	**$285-$300**
Gray	**$255-$270**
Ivory	**$190-$210**
Light Green	**$140-$160**
Red	**$190-$225**
Rose	**$285-$300**
Turquoise	**$150-$160**
Yellow	**$145-$160**
Medium Green	**$1,250-$1,395**

Covered casserole in light green. **$140-$160**

Covered casserole in rose. **$285-$300**

Covered casserole in yellow. **$145-$160**

Covered casserole in red. **$190-$225**

Covered casseroles in red, **$190-$225,** and yellow, **$145-$160**.

Coffeepots

Coffeepot

Dimensions: 10-1/2" by 8" by 4-1/2" (lid)
Production Dates: 1936 to 1959

The coffeepot seems to have sold well in the early years of Fiesta, judging from the number that have survived. The same cannot be said for the colors the 1950s. Forest green, chartreuse, and rose are all harder to find, but it is the last color of the 1950s, gray, that tops the list. The coffeepot held seven cups and can be marked "Fiesta/HLC USA" or "Fiesta/Made in USA." Red was discontinued in 1944; examples in gray bring a premium.

Degree of Difficulty: 2-3

Chartreuse	$410-$460	Light Green	$195-$220
Cobalt Blue	$238-$270	Red	$250-$275
Forest Green	$458-$495	Rose	$475-$520
Gray	$625-$665	Turquoise	$185-$210
Ivory	$230-$255	Yellow	$185-$218

Coffeepot in cobalt blue.
$238-$270

Coffeepot in red.
$250-$275

Demitasse coffeepot

Also called "After Dinner" or "A.D.," dimensions: 7-1/2" by 7" by 3-1/2" (lid)

Production Dates: 1936 to 1943

Designed to be used for an after dinner beverage (Turkish coffee, demitasse or even hot chocolate). With the exception of the handle, this piece is a scaled-down version of the coffeepot. The vent hole in the cover was put in by hand. You may find a cover without the hole added, or sometimes the vent hole may be in a different part of the cover. The demitasse coffeepot is marked "Fiesta/HLC USA."

Degree of Difficulty: 3-4

Cobalt Blue	$490-$520	Red	$550-$575
Light Green	$475-$525	Turquoise	$650-$695
Ivory	$510-$550	Yellow	$450-$500

Demitasse coffeepot and cups and saucers in original colors.

Demitasse coffeepot in red, **$550-$575,** and turquoise, **$650-$695**.

Demitasse coffeepot in light green. **$475-$525**

Demitasse coffeepot in yellow. **$450-$500**

Comports

Comport

Called the 12" comport, dimensions: 12-1/2" by 3-1/2"
Production Dates: 1936 to 1946

A multi-purpose item, this piece could be used as a centerpiece bowl along with either of the candleholders, or as a salad bowl. The foot adds elegance to an otherwise utilitarian bowl. These comports may be found unmarked or with a "Genuine Fiesta" stamp. Production of red was halted in 1944.

Degree of Difficulty: 3

Cobalt Blue	$175-$195	Red	$190-$200
Ivory	$170-$190	Turquoise	$160-$175
Light Green	$150-$165	Yellow	$175-$180

Comport in cobalt blue. **$175-$195**

Comport in ivory. **$170-$190**

Comport in red. **$190-$200**

Sweets comport

Dimensions: 5-1/8" by 3-1/2"
Production Dates: 1936 to 1947
The addition of the tall foot adds to the charm of this piece, which is great for candy or nuts. It seemed to have sold well during its 11 years of production. Sweets comports may be found with an "HLCo USA" stamp, but they are seldom marked. Production of red examples was halted in 1944.

Degree of Difficulty: 2

Cobalt Blue	$85-$95	Red	$100-$115
Ivory	$80-$95	Turquoise	$80-$90
Light Green	$80-$85	Yellow	$70-$79

Sweets comports in yellow, **$70-$79,** and light green, **$80-$85.**

Sweets comport in cobalt blue. **$85-$95**

Creamers & Sugar Bowls

Ring-handle creamer

Dimensions: 5-7/8" by 3" by 3-5/8"
Production Dates: 1938 to 1969
The ring-handle creamer replaced the stick-handle creamer. The body is the same as the stick-handle creamer, but the handle portion is different. With the ring handle opposite the spout, left-handed people could use this creamer with ease. Production of red examples was halted in 1944 and resumed in 1959.

Degree of Difficulty: 1

Chartreuse	$42-$46	Red	$36-$41
Cobalt Blue	$32-$39	Rose	$40-$50
Forest Green	$40-$44	Turquoise	$23-$28
Gray	$40-$50	Yellow	$26-$29
Light Green	$26-$29	Medium Green	$120-$135
Ivory	$32-$38		

Ring-handle creamer with covered sugar bowl in medium green. **$120-$135** for the creamer, **$175-$195** for the sugar bowl.

Ring-handle creamer in light green. **$26-$29**

Ring-handle creamer in rose. **$40-$50**

Stick-handle creamer

Dimensions: 4-5/8" by 3" by 3-5/8" without handle
Production Dates: 1936 to 1938
Produced for less than three years, this creamer was one of the first items to be restyled. The creamer is easy for right-handed people to use, but is difficult for left-handed people to use. The stick-handle creamer, which matched the after-dinner—or demitasse—coffeepot, was succeeded by the more versatile ring-handle creamer. It bears an impressed "HLC USA" mark.

Degree of Difficulty: 2-3

Cobalt Blue	$60-$68	Red	$65-$72
Ivory	$62-$68	Turquoise	$75-$80
Light Green	$45-$49	Yellow	$45-$49

Stick-handle creamer in ivory.
$62-$68

Stick-handle creamer in yellow.
$45-$49

Sugar bowl

Also called the covered sugar. Dimensions: 3-3/4" without handles by 5" with cover
Production Dates: 1936 to 1969

A standard item in dinnerware sets, the sugar bowl enjoyed a 33-year run. The covered sugar underwent an early design change just months after introduction. Check the inside bottom of the sugar bowl. Sugar bowls with flat bottoms are hard to find as they were only made at the beginning of 1936. After a few months, the inside of the sugar bowl was rounded. The sugar bowl can be marked either "Fiesta/HLC U.S.A." or "Made in U.S.A." Those in 1950s colors may have a foot that is slightly less flared. Production of red examples was halted in 1944 and resumed in 1959.

Degree of Difficulty: 1-2 for all colors except medium green, which ranks 2-3.

Covered sugar bowl in medium green. **$175-$195**

Covered sugar in turquoise. **$49-$58**

Chartreuse	**$69-$77**
Cobalt Blue	**$58-$70**
Forest Green	**$72-$78**
Gray	**$68-$75**
Ivory	**$58-$70**
Light Green	**$48-$55**
Red	**$60-$72**
Rose	**$70-$78**
Turquoise	**$49-$58**
Yellow	**$48-$57**
Medium Green	**$175-$195**

Covered sugar bowl, **$60-$72,** and stick-handle creamer in red, **$65-$72**.

Covered sugar bowl in yellow, **$48-$57,** stick handle creamer in red, **$65-$72,** and ring-handle creamer in light green, **$26-$29**.

Cups & Mugs

Demitasse cup and saucer

Also called "After Dinner" or "A.D."
Dimensions: Cup, 2-1/2" by 2-1/2" without handle by 2-1/2", and saucer, 5-1/4" diameter by 3/4"
Production Dates: 1936 to 1959

Designed to go along with the after dinner or demitasse coffeepot, this cup looks like a scaled-down version of a teacup or eggcup with a stick handle. Before Starbucks, after dinner demitasse or Turkish coffee was the rage in the late 1930s-early 1940s. These cups are rarely marked, and they also vary in style details: Cups made before late 1937 have a flat inner bottom; those made after that time have a rounded inner bottom. Early demitasse saucers also have two rings around the base or foot; examples after 1937 have a single ring and are usually stamped "Genuine Fiesta." Production of red examples was halted in 1944.

Degree of Difficulty: 2-3 for the original six colors, 3-4 for colors of the 1950s.

Chartreuse	$495-$520/pair	Light Green	$78-$80/pair
Cobalt Blue	$80-$92/pair	Red	$82-$95/pair
Forest Green	$490-$520/pair	Rose	$490-$515/pair
Gray	$495-$535/pair	Turquoise	$80-$85/pair
Ivory	$80-$90/pair	Yellow	$60-$79/pair

Demitasse cup and saucer in light green. **$78-$80/pair**

Demitasse cup and saucer in cobalt blue. **$80-$92/pair**

Demitasse cup and saucer in yellow. **$60-$79/pair**

Demitasse cups and saucers in ivory, **$80-$90/pair,** and red, **$82-$95/pair.**

Eggcup

Dimensions: 3-3/8" by 3-1/8"
Production Dates: 1936 to 1959
This eggcup was designed for a poached egg rather than in the traditional design to hold an egg to be eaten from the shell. Often unmarked, it can also have a "Made in USA" impressed mark. Production of red examples was halted in 1944.

Degree of Difficulty: 2-3 for the original six colors; 3-4 for colors of the 1950s.

Chartreuse	$148-$160	Light Green	$55-$66
Cobalt Blue	$68-$76	Red	$70-$85
Forest Green	$150-$165	Rose	$150-$165
Gray	$160-$165	Turquoise	$56-$65
Ivory	$66-$72	Yellow	$56-$64

Eggcup in yellow. **$56-$64**

Eggcup in turquoise. **$56-$65**

Eggcup in ivory. **$66-$72**

Eggcup in light green. **$55-$66**

Eggcup in red. **$70-$85**

Teacup and saucer

Dimensions: Cup, 3-1/2" by 2-3/4" without handle, and saucer, 6" diameter by 3/4"

Production Dates: 1936 to 1969

In the product line for more than 33 years, the teacup and saucer are not hard to find. No doubt it was a good seller. The teacup and saucer come in three variations: Cups made up to 1937 have a flat inner bottom and rings inside the rim; saucers have five rings around the base or foot; neither is marked. Cups made after 1937 have a rounded inner bottom and inner rim rings, while the saucers have a single wide ring under the rim, and a "Genuine Fiesta" stamp. In the 1960s, the cup was slightly enlarged and redesigned without a turned foot or rings inside the rim; the saucers are slightly deeper with a double band of rings under the rim, and a "Genuine Fiesta" stamp.

Degree of Difficulty: 1-2 for the six original colors; 2 for the colors of the 1950s; and 2-3 for medium green.

Teacup and saucer in medium green.
$60-$70/pair

Chartreuse	**$40-$45/pair**
Cobalt Blue	**$36-$44/pair**
Forest Green	**$44-$49/pair**
Gray	**$36-$43/pair**
Ivory	**$35-$43/pair**
Light Green	**$29-$34/pair**
Red	**$40-$50/pair**
Rose	**$42-$51/pair**
Turquoise	**$34-$38/pair**
Yellow	**$29-$33/pair**
Medium Green	**$60-$70/pair**

Teacup and saucer in forest green.
$44-$49/pair

Teacup and saucer in gray. **$36-$43/pair**

Teacup and saucer in rose. **$42-$51/pair**

Teacup and saucer in cobalt blue.
$36-$44/pair

Teacup and saucer in
ivory. **$35-$43/pair**

Teacup and saucer in yellow.
$29-$33/pair

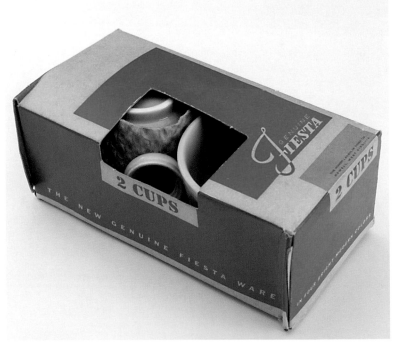

Unopened boxed set of two teacups in yellow. Boxes can double or triple the overall value of the piece.

Tom & Jerry mug

Dimensions: 3-1/8" by 4-3/8"
Production Dates: 1936 until 1969

The Tom & Jerry is a hot alcoholic drink made with eggs, sugar, and whiskey. The Tom & Jerry mug is one of two Fiesta pieces that do not have the familiar band of rings for which Fiesta is famous. (The other item is the syrup pitcher.) Today's collectors use this mug for coffee or tea. You will often find the Tom & Jerry mug in white with "Tom & Jerry" in gold, part of the Tom & Jerry set that also included a footed salad bowl used to hold the beverage. When marked, the mugs bear the "Genuine Fiesta" stamp. Production of red examples was halted in 1944 and resumed in 1959.

Degree of Difficulty: 2 for all colors except medium green, which is a 3.

Chartreuse	**$84-$88**
Cobalt Blue	**$75-$82**
Forest Green	**$80-$85**
Gray	**$82-$86**
Light Green	**$65-$69**
Ivory	**$76-$84**
Red	**$79-$88**
Rose	**$86-$89**
Turquoise	**$60-$65**
Yellow	**$65-$68**
Medium Green	**$125-$140**

Tom & Jerry mug in medium green.
$125-$140

Three Tom & Jerry mugs in yellow, **$65-$68,** light green, **$65-$69**, and red, **$79-$88**.

Three Tom & Jerry mugs in forest green, **$80-$85,** gray, **$82-$86**, and chartreuse, **$84-$88**.

Tom & Jerry mugs in the original six colors.

Marmalade Jar

Dimensions: 3-1/8" by 4-1/16" with lid
Production Dates: 1936 to 1946
Production of Red examples was halted in 1944. Red marmalade jars are harder to find than the other colors, probably due to the fact that their production run was two years shorter than the other colors. The slot in the lid, for a spoon, was hand-cut, so slot sizes vary from lid to lid. Marmalade jars are marked on the base "Fiesta/HLC USA."

Degree of Difficulty: 3-4

Cobalt Blue	$335-$360	Red	$350-$395
Ivory	$340-$365	Turquoise	$325-$360
Light Green	$300-$350	Yellow	$315-$355

Marmalades in red, **$350-$395,** and yellow, **$315-$355**, including glass spoons with colored tips.

Marmalade jar in ivory. **$340-$365**

Marmalade jar in light green, **$300-$350,** with covered mustard in ivory, **$280-$300**.

Covered Mustard

Dimensions: 2-1/2" by 3-1/16" with lid
Production Dates: 1936 to 1946

The covered mustard is not an easy piece to find. Many lids are found cracked or chipped because the covered mustard is a small item with a lid that's difficult to pick up by its finial. The lid was made in one piece, unlike the marmalade jar, which had a hand-applied finial. The mustard is easily distinguished from the marmalade jar by its smaller size and the tapered—rather than flaring—knob on the lid. Like the marmalade cover, the mustard cover's slot for the spoon was cut out by hand, so expect some variations in the slot's size. The covered mustard is rarely marked. Production of red examples was halted in 1944.

Degree of Difficulty: 3-4

Cobalt Blue	**$280-$300**	Red	**$290-$315**
Ivory	**$280-$300**	Turquoise	**$275-$285**
Light Green	**$250-$265**	Yellow	**$255-$270**

Three mustards in yellow, **$255-$270,** light green, **$250-$265**, and turquoise,
$275-$285.

Two mustards in red, **$290-$315,** and ivory, **$280-$300**.

Pitchers & Jugs

Disk water pitcher

Dimensions: 7-1/2" by 8-3/4" by 5"
Production Dates: 1938 to 1969
If there is one piece of Fiesta that sums up the feel of the line, it is this pitcher. Flat, yet three-dimensional, this piece is a striking addition to any table. With a capacity of 70 ounces, the disk water pitcher was in production for almost 31 years. It is also part of the post-1986 line in contemporary colors. Production of red examples was halted in 1944 and resumed in 1959. Pitchers by other manufacturers in this shape are common, so look for the "Fiesta/Made in USA" impressed mark.

Degree of Difficulty: 1-2 for original colors, 3-4 for colors of the 1950s, and 5 for medium green.

Chartreuse	$235-$260	Red	$160-$180
Cobalt Blue	$155-$175	Rose	$225-$265
Forest Green	$225-$265	Turquoise	$115-$125
Gray	$225-$250	Yellow	$115-$125
Ivory	$155-$170	Medium Green	$1,500-$1,600
Light Green	$110-$120		

Disk water pitcher in cobalt blue. **$155-$175**

Disk water pitcher in light green. **$110-$120**

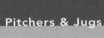

Disk water pitcher in ivory. **$155-$170**

Disk water pitcher in medium green. **$1,500-$1,600**

Disk water pitcher in red. **$160-$180**

Disk water pitcher in rose. **$225-$265**

Disk water pitcher in turquoise. **$115-$125**

Disk water pitcher in yellow. **$115-$125**

Ice pitcher

Dimensions: 6-1/2" by 9-3/4" by 6-1/2"
Production Dates: 1936 to 1946
Many a novice collector has mistaken this piece for one of Fiesta's two teapots. If you look closely, the ice pitcher resembles the bottom of a large teapot, but with a medium teapot handle. Even though this piece was in production for more than 10 years, it is not easy to find. Often incorrectly called the "ice lip" pitcher, it is marked "HLC USA." Production of red examples was halted in 1944.

Degree of Difficulty: 2-3

Cobalt Blue	**$140-$155**	Red	**$145-$170**
Light Green	**$140-$150**	Turquoise	**$145-$165**
Ivory	**$140-$160**	Yellow	**$135-$145**

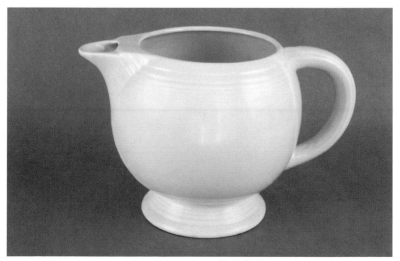

Ice pitcher in ivory. **$140-$160**

Ice pitcher in light green. **$140-$150**

Ice pitcher in yellow. **$135-$145**

Syrup pitcher with "DripCut" top

Dimensions: 5-3/4", including top, by 3-5/8" without handle
Production Dates: 1938 to 1940
In production for only two years, the syrup pitcher is not easy to find. The plastic lids were made by the DripCut Corporation to match Fiesta and another Homer Laughlin Co. dinnerware line. DripCut tops are found in the original six colors, with slight color variations because of age. The plastic lids tend to fade if left near the sun. There were two styles of lids, so be careful if you are purchasing a syrup pitcher top or bottom without the other. The pitcher body was also used as a lamp base and as a container for Dutchess Tea.

Degree of Difficulty: 3-4

Cobalt Blue	**$420-$440**
Ivory	**$420-$440**
Light Green	**$350-$365**
Red	**$425-$450**
Turquoise	**$400-$430**
Yellow	**$350-$365**

DripCut syrup pitcher in cobalt blue with a blue top, marked Fiesta. **$420-$440**

DripCut syrup pitcher in ivory. **$420-$440**

Two-pint jug

Dimensions: 4-1/4" by 8-1/2" by 5-1/2"
Production Dates: 1936 to 1959

The two-pint jug was originally planned to be part of a five-piece set of jugs, with sizes ranging from one-half cup to two pints. The two-pint jug was the only size produced. It may be marked "HLC USA" with a "5" near the Fiesta logo, or "Made in USA" without the number.

Degree of Difficulty: 2-3 (There is not much difference in the degree of difficulty between the original colors and the colors of the 1950s.)

Chartreuse	$130-$140	Light Green	$90-$95
Cobalt Blue	$110-$125	Red	$115-$135
Forest Green	$135-$140	Rose	$150-$160
Gray	$155-$160	Turquoise	$90-$95
Ivory	$110-$115	Yellow	$85-$90

Two-pint jug in light green, **$90-$95,** with ice pitcher in ivory, **$140-$160.**

Two-pint jug in chartreuse. **$130-$140**

Two-pint jug in rose. **$150-$160**

Two-pint jug in red. **$115-$135**

Two-pint jugs in turquoise, **$90-$95,** and red, **$115-$135**.

Plates

6" Plate

Dimensions: 6-1/2" diameter by 5/8" thick

Production Dates: 1936 to 1969

Also known as a bread and butter plate, this item was in the line until it was restyled in 1969. Along with the 7" and 9" plates, the 6" plate is very easy to locate, thus the lower prices. Most 6" plates have a "Genuine Fiesta" stamp. Production of red examples was halted in 1944 and resumed in 1959.

Degree of Difficulty: 1

Chartreuse	$9-$11
Cobalt Blue	$7-$8
Forest Green	$9-$10
Gray	$10-$11
Ivory	$6-$7
Light Green	$6-$7
Red	$8-$9
Rose	$9-$11
Turquoise	$6-$7
Yellow	$6-$7
Medium Green	$21-$28

6" plate in gray. **$10-$11**

6" and 7" plates in red. **$8-$9** and **$12-$15**, respectively

6" and 7" plates in medium green. **$21-$28** and **$40-$42**, respectively

7" Plate

Dimensions: Actual diameter 7-1/2" by 5/8" thick
Production Dates: 1936 until 1969
Often called a salad plate or cake plate, this item was in the Fiesta line for 33 years. It often bears the "Genuine Fiesta" stamp when marked. Production of red examples was halted in 1944 and resumed in 1959.

Degree of Difficulty: 1

Chartreuse	**$14-$16**
Cobalt Blue	**$10-$12**
Forest Green	**$15-$17**
Gray	**$15-$17**
Ivory	**$10-$12**
Light Green	**$10-$11**
Red	**$12-$15**
Rose	**$15-$17**
Turquoise	**$9-$10**
Yellow	**$9-$10**
Medium Green	**$40-$42**

7" plate in medium green. **$40-$42**

6" and 7" plates in ivory. **$6-$7** and **$10-$12**, respectively

Unopened original box of Fiesta containing two salad plates in yellow. Boxes can double or triple the overall value of the pieces they contain.

7" plates (top to bottom): yellow, **$9-$10,** turquoise, **$9-$10**, red, **$12-$15**, forest green, **$15-$17**, light green, **$10-$11**, chartreuse, **$14-$16**, cobalt blue, **$10-$12**, rose, **$15-$17**, and ivory, **$10-$12**.

7" plates in light green, cobalt blue, turquoise, yellow, and red.

9" Plate

Dimensions: Actual diameter 9-1/2" by 3/4" thick
Production Dates: 1936 to 1969
What was the very first item that was modeled for the Fiesta line? If you said the 9" plate, move to the head of the class. Nine-inch plates were often included in boxed sets of Fiesta dishes, perhaps sold as a luncheon set. Because of this, 9" plates are far easier to locate today than the 10" dinner plates. The 9" plate often bears the "Genuine Fiesta" stamp when marked. Production of red examples was halted in 1944 and resumed in 1959.

Degree of Difficulty: 1

Chartreuse	$25-$28
Cobalt Blue	$17-$19
Forest Green	$21-$24
Gray	$25-$28
Ivory	$17-$18
Light Green	$12-$15
Red	$18-$20
Rose	$26-$29
Turquoise	$13-$17
Yellow	$12-$15
Medium Green	$48-$60

9" plate in medium green. **$48-$60** (Note color and ring pattern variation between this and the 10" plate.)

Place setting with 9" plate, teacup, and saucer, and 6" and 7" plates in yellow. (Note color differences in smaller plates.)
$56-$65/set

Place setting with 9" plate, teacup, and saucer, and 6" and 7" plates in light green.
$57-$67/set

Place setting with 9" plate, teacup, and saucer, and 6" and 7" plates in red. **$78-$94/set**

Place setting with 9" plate, teacup, and saucer, and 6" and 7" plates in cobalt blue. **$70-$83/set**

Place setting with 9" plate, teacup, and saucer, and 6" and 7" plates in ivory. (Note color differences in smaller plates.) **$68-$80/set**

Place setting with 9" plate, teacup, and saucer, and 6" and 7" plates in turquoise. (Note ring pattern variation in large plate.) **$58-$65/set**

Place setting with 9" plate, teacup, and saucer, and 6" and 7" plates in medium green. **$169-$200/set**

Place setting with 9" plate, teacup, and saucer, and 6" and 7" plates in gray. **$86-$99/set**

Place setting with 9" plate, teacup, and saucer, and 6" and 7" plates in rose. **$92-$108/ set**

Place setting with 9" plate, teacup, and saucer, and 6" and 7" plates in chartreuse. **$88-$100/set**

Place setting with 9" plate, teacup, and saucer, and 6" and 7" plates in forest green. **$89-$100/set**

9" plate in red. **$18-$20**

9" plate in cobalt blue.
$17-$19

9" plate in yellow.
$12-$15

9" plate in turquoise.
$13-$17

9" plate in light green.
$12-$15

10" Plate

Dimensions: Actual diameter 10-1/2" by 3/4" thick
Production Dates: 1936 to 1969
A bit more difficult to find, 10" dinner plates can really enhance a basic dinnerware service. Before you purchase a plate, check for scratches. The 10" plate often bears the "Genuine Fiesta" stamp when marked. Production of red examples was halted in 1944 and resumed in 1959.

Degree of Difficulty: 1-2

Chartreuse	**$50-$55**	Red	**$40-$48**
Cobalt Blue	**$40-$46**	Rose	**$50-$55**
Forest Green	**$50-$56**	Turquoise	**$30-$35**
Gray	**$45-$50**	Yellow	**$30-$45**
Ivory	**$40-$46**	Medium Green	**$125-$145**
Light Green	**$30-$39**		

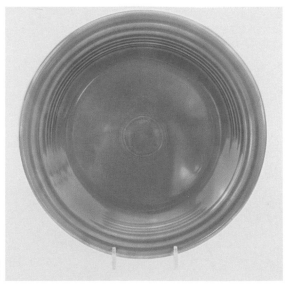

10" plate in medium green. **$125-$145**

10" plate in cobalt blue. **$40-$46**

10" plate in light green. **$30-$39**

10" plate in yellow. **$30-$45**

10" plate in ivory. **$40-$46**

10" plate in red.
$40-$48

10" plate in
turquoise.
$30-$35

Cake plate

Dimensions: 10-3/8" diameter by 5/8" thick
Production Dates: Approximately six months in 1937.
One of the hardest pieces of Fiesta to locate, the cake plate is often mistaken for a dinner plate and may be hidden in a stack of dinner plates at an antiques store. Several bands of rings appear on the back of the cake plate, the most of any single Fiesta piece. For many collectors, the cake plate and the nestled bowl lids are the centerpieces of their Fiesta collections. Some cake plates have been found with a "Royal Chrome Colored Ovenware" sticker and may have had a separate pierced metal base.

Degree of Difficulty: 5

Cobalt Blue	**$1,300-$1,450**
Light Green	**$1,000-$1,200**
Ivory	**$1,425-$1,495**
Red	**$1,400-$1,495**
Yellow	**$1,200-$1,300**

Top, bottom, and side views of a cake plate in yellow, **$1,200-$1,300.** Notice the back of the plate is full of rings, unlike the back of a dinner plate, and it is completely flat.

Calendar plate

Dimensions: 9" and 10" diameter
Production Dates: 1954 to 1955
Over the years, many china companies have made calendar plates, and the Homer Laughlin Co. was no exception. The company used various blanks (undecorated plates) on which to display the complete calendar for the year. During 1954 and 1955, the blanks that were used were Fiesta plates. A 10" ivory Fiesta plate was used in 1954. In 1955 both 9" and 10" Fiesta plates were utilized. The 10" plates were available in light green, yellow, and ivory. The 9" plates seem to have been made only in ivory. There is no clear explanation for why these plates were made for only two years. None have a manufacturer's mark.

Degree of Difficulty: 2-3

Light Green, Ivory, and Yellow   **$40-$50**

13" Chop plate

Dimensions: Actual diameter 12-1/2" by 1-1/8" thick
Production Dates: 1936 to 1969
A large round plate like the dinner plate, only larger, this piece may or may not have two different footed rings on the underside. Some 13" chop plates have been found with a metal Lazy Susan turner. The metal piece fits perfectly under the chop plate, turning it into a great buffet server. The 13" chop plate is often stamped "Genuine Fiesta," though some are unmarked. A raffia-wrapped metal handle was offered as a special promotion and could be clipped onto the plate. (See Promotional Items)

Degree of Difficulty: 1-2 for all colors except medium green, which ranks 3-4.

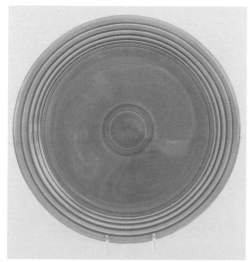

Chartreuse	$85-$90
Cobalt Blue	$50-$55
Forest Green	$90-$95
Gray	$90-$98
Ivory	$49-$55
Light Green	$40-$50
Red	$50-$58
Rose	$95-$105
Turquoise	$45-$49
Yellow	$40-$48
Medium Green	$400-$475

13" chop plate in medium green. **$400-$475**

13" chop plate in yellow.
$40-$48

13" chop plate in
turquoise. **$45-$49**

13" chop plate in rose. **$95-$105**

13" chop plate in light green. **$40-$50**

13" chop plate in ivory. **$49-$55**

15" Chop plate

Dimensions: Actual diameter 14-1/4" by 1-1/8" thick
Production Dates: 1936 tol 1959
The 15" chop plate is excellent for serving a large portion of meat, such as a turkey or ham. Unfortunately, even without anything on it, the piece is heavy. It's a great addition to a buffet table, but should not be passed at a sit-down dinner because of its weight. Fifteen-inch chop plates have a double foot ring and are stamped "Genuine Fiesta." These plates often have significant surface scratching, which is most evident on dark glazes.

Degree of Difficulty: 1-2 for original colors, and 2-3 for colors of the 1950s.

Chartreuse	**$100-$120**
Cobalt Blue	**$84-$92**
Forest Green	**$100-$120**
Gray	**$110-$120**
Ivory	**$80-$90**
Light Green	**$60-$75**
Red	**$85-$99**
Rose	**$100-$125**
Turquoise	**$64-$70**
Yellow	**$58-$70**

15" chop plate in ivory, **$80-$90,** with light green bud vase, **$85-$94**.

15" chop plate in red, **$85-$99,** with yellow bud vase, **$85-$92**.

15" chop plate in cobalt blue, **$84-$92,** with ivory bud vase, **$100-$120**.

10-1/2" Compartment plate

Dimensions: 10-1/2" diameter by 7/8" thick
Production Dates: 1937 to 1959
This item appeared in the Fiesta line approximately 15 months after the introduction of Fiesta. The 10-1/2" compartment plate replaced the 12" version because it was much easier to hold and it weighed less. It is routinely stamped "Genuine Fiesta."

Degree of Difficulty: 2

Chartreuse	$75-$82	Light Green	$40-$48
Cobalt Blue	$50-$60	Red	$65-$75
Forest Green	$85-$95	Rose	$75-$85
Gray	$80-$85	Turquoise	$45-$55
Ivory	$50-$64	Yellow	$40-$48

10-1/2" compartment plate in red. **$65-$75**

10-1/2" compartment plate in red, **$65-$75,** and 12" compartment plate in light green, **$58-$65**.

12" Compartment plate

Dimensions: Actual diameter 11-3/4" by 1-1/8" thick
Production Dates: 1936 to early 1937
This piece is also known as a grill plate. It was popular in the 1930s
to offer a grill plate in a dinnerware line. Due to the heavy nature of
this piece, there are two double feet underneath. This prevented
a tendency for the plate to warp when it was fired in the kiln. The
12" compartment plate is not marked, and the compartments are
slightly shallower than the 10-1/2" size.

Degree of Difficulty: 2

Cobalt Blue	**$72-$80**
Ivory	**$70-$78**
Light Green	**$58-$65**
Red	**$75-$80**
Yellow	**$58-$65**

12" compartment plate in cobalt blue. **$72-$80**

12" compartment plate in red. **$75-$80**

12" compartment plate in light green. **$58-$65**

Deep plate

Dimensions: 8-1/2" diameter by 1-1/2" thick
Production Dates: 1936 to 1969
Also known as a rimmed soup bowl, this item was in production for approximately 33 years and sold quite well, as is evident by the number of them on the market today. Bowls were popular during the Depression because soup was a hearty, filling, and inexpensive way to feed a family. Most dinnerware lines of the 1930s had several size bowls, from dessert to fruit, and from cream soups to large, hearty appetite bowls. The deep plate is stamped "Genuine Fiesta." Production of red examples was halted in 1944 and resumed in 1959.

Degree of Difficulty: 1-2

Chartreuse	**$50-$55**
Cobalt Blue	**$60-$70**
Forest Green	**$50-$56**
Gray	**$52-$58**
Ivory	**$58-$68**
Light Green	**$45-$56**
Red	**$60-$70**
Rose	**$55-$60**
Turquoise	**$45-$54**
Yellow	**$45-$55**
Medium Green	**$135-$150**

Deep plate in medium green. **$135-$150**

Deep plate in red. **$60-$70**

Deep plate in turquoise.
$45-$54

Deep plate in cobalt blue.
$60-$70

Deep plate in ivory. **$58-$68**

Deep plate in an unusually strong light green glaze. **$45-$56**

Deep plate in a heavy light green glaze, **$45-$56,** next to a teacup in medium green.

Deep plate in yellow.
$45-$55

Deep plate in
chartreuse. **$50-$55**

Deep plate in rose. **$55-$60**

Platters

Oval platter

Dimensions: 12-3/4" long before 1947; 12-1/2" long after 1947; 1-1/2" thick

Production Dates: 1938 to 1969

The oval platter was another popular item for Fiesta as well as other dinnerware lines. The angled sides made this an easy item to pass from person to person at the table, as juices would not drip off. It is commonly marked with a "Genuine Fiesta" stamp. Production of red examples was halted in 1944 and resumed in 1959.

Degree of Difficulty: 2

Chartreuse	$50-$60	Red	$50-$55
Cobalt Blue	$48-$53	Rose	$53-$59
Forest Green	$55-$65	Turquoise	$40-$48
Gray	$58-$65	Yellow	$40-$46
Light Green	$40-$46	Medium Green	$175-$210
Ivory	$45-$50		

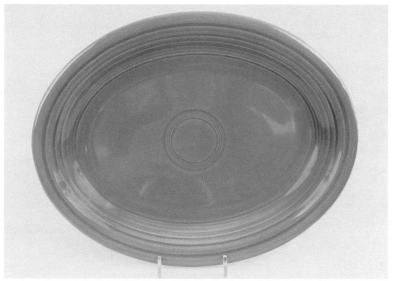

Oval platter in medium green. **$175-$210**

Oval platter in turquoise. **$40-$48**

Oval platter in chartreuse. **$50-$60**

Oval platters in cobalt blue and yellow. **$48-$53** and **$40-$46**, respectively

Oval platter in ivory. **$45-$50**

Oval platter in light green.
$40-$46

Salt & Pepper Shakers

Dimensions: 2-3/8" by 2-3/4"

Production Dates: 1936 to 1969

These salt and pepper shakers represent great art deco design. The addition of a foot on a sphere shape gives this piece a classic look. The holes in the top are generally larger for the salt shaker and smaller for the pepper shaker. Salt and pepper shakers were originally available separately and seldom marked. They are also available in Fiesta Ironstone and Amberstone colors. After 1967, the pepper shaker was made with six holes rather than seven. They came with cork stoppers. Salt and pepper shakers are not too difficult to locate, except for examples in medium green. Production of red examples was halted in 1944 and resumed in 1959.

Degree of Difficulty: 1 for the original colors, 1-2 for colors of the 1950s, and 3-4 for medium green.

Chartreuse	$50-$55/pair	Red	$30-$35/pair
Cobalt Blue	$30-$34/pair	Rose	$48-$52/pair
Forest Green	$50-$55/pair	Turquoise	$25-$29/pair
Gray	$48-$52/pair	Yellow	$25-$29/pair
Ivory	$29-$35/pair	Medium Green	$200-$210/pair
Light Green	$25-$29/pair		

Shakers in medium green. **$200-$210/pair**

Shakers in cobalt blue. **$30-$34/pair**

Shakers in yellow. **$25-$29/pair**

Shakers in light green. **$25-$29/pair**

Shakers in red.
$30-$35/pair

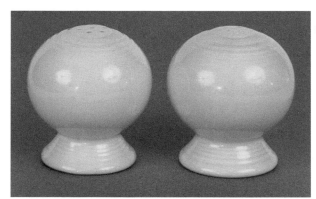

Shakers in ivory.
$29-$35/pair

Shakers in turquoise (note color variation).
$25-$29/pair

Shakers in
chartreuse.
$50-$55/pair

Shakers in gray.
$48-$52/pair

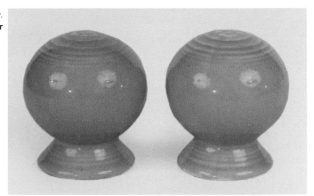

Shakers in rose.
$48-$52/pair

Sauceboats

Dimensions: 4-7/8" by 8" by 4-1/2"
Production Dates: 1938 to 1969

The sauceboat came out in 1938, but the under plate, which looks like a mini oval platter, was not produced until 1969. For those of you without an underliner, a gravy ladle works well and prevents dripping. This piece was part of the vintage line (marked "Fiesta/HLC U.S.A." or "Fiesta/Made in U.S.A."), and is available in the Ironstone colors (unmarked) and in the Post-'86 line. Production of vintage red was halted in 1944 and resumed in 1959.

Degree of Difficulty: 1-2 for all colors other than medium green, which ranks 3-4.

Chartreuse	$70-$80	Light Green	$50-$60
Cobalt Blue	$70-$79	Ivory	$70-$79
Forest Green	$72-$84	Turquoise	$50-$54
Gray	$70-$82	Yellow	$50-$54
Red	$75-$89	Medium Green	$195-$240
Rose	$75-$85		

Sauceboat in medium green. **$195-$240**

Sauceboat in cobalt blue. **$70-$79**

Sauceboat and stand in red. **$75-$89**

Sauceboat in ivory. **$70-$79**

Sauceboat in yellow.
$50-$54

Sauceboat in turquoise.
$50-$54

Sauceboat in gray.
$70-$82

Sauceboat in forest green. **$72-$84**

Sauceboat in light green, **$50-$60,** with compote in cobalt blue, **$175-$195**.

Teapots
Medium teapot

Dimensions: 8-1/2" by 5-1/8" with lid, by 5-5/8"

Production Dates: 1937 to 1969

The medium teapot made its debut one year after the introduction of Fiesta. While somewhat similar to the large teapot, there are several differences. On the medium teapot, the lid finial does not flare; the spout is longer and arched; and the handle is C-shaped, rather than a ring. The vent holes were put in by hand, so watch for some variations on the lid—some lids may not even have a vent hole. Made for 32 years, medium teapots in the original colors are much easier to find than large teapots, which were produced for only 11 years. Production of red examples was halted in 1944 and resumed in 1959.

Degree of Difficulty: 2 for the original colors and 3 for the colors of the 1950s and medium green.

Chartreuse	$300-$325	Turquoise	$175-$200
Cobalt Blue	$210-$235	Yellow	$160-$180
Forest Green	$325-$340	Medium Green	$1,475-$1,595
Gray	$330-$350		
Ivory	$195-$220		
Light Green	$160-$175		
Red	$200-$230		
Rose	$295-$325		

Medium teapot in
medium green.
$1,475-$1,595

Medium teapot in red.
$200-$230

Medium teapot in turquoise.
$175-$200

Medium teapot in ivory. **$195-$220**

Medium teapot in yellow.
$160-$180

Medium teapot in rose. **$295-$325**

Large teapot

Dimensions: 9-1/4" by 6-3/4" with lid, by 6-1/8"
Production Dates: 1936 to 1946
This is one of the many items that were in the line when Fiesta debuted in January 1936. It is not known why a smaller-sized teapot (called the medium teapot) with a different handle was introduced a year later, but the shear bulk of the large teapot when it is full, along with its somewhat awkward ring handle, may be the reason. Although a beautiful design, it is difficult to pour when filled with eight cups of hot water. The large teapot may be marked either "Fiesta/HLC USA" or "Made in USA." The lids typically have a steam vent hole.

Degree of Difficulty: 2-3

Cobalt Blue	**$300-$325**
Ivory	**$285-$310**
Light Green	**$275-$295**
Red	**$300-$325**
Turquoise	**$295-$315**
Yellow	**$290-$300**

Large teapot in yellow.
$290-$300

Trays

Relish tray

Tray (with five inserts) overall dimensions: 10-7/8" by 1-1/2".
Production Dates: 1936-1946
The Fiesta relish tray (the base, four quarter-round inserts, and a round center section) was shipped from Homer Laughlin Co. in one color. Some retailers and buyers mixed up their colors to create various color schemes. If buying an incomplete tray, be careful: The quarter-round inserts come in two sizes, and when mixed, will not fit snugly around the center section. The tray is typically marked "Fiesta/HLC USA" while the inserts may be unmarked, or marked "Genuine Fiesta/Made in USA." Production of red was discontinued in 1944.

Degree of Difficulty: 2-3

Cobalt Blue	$300-$335/set	Red	$300-$325/set
Ivory	$300-$325/set	Turquoise	$300-$340/set
Light Green	$295-$310/set	Yellow	$290-$310/set

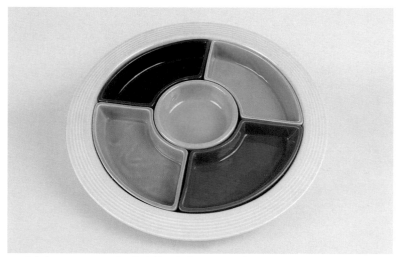

Relish tray in ivory with cobalt blue, light green, red, turquoise, and yellow inserts.

Relish tray and inserts in light green, as it would have come from the factory.
$295-$310/set

Relish tray with removable metal handle.

Relish tray in light green, cobalt blue, yellow, ivory, and turquoise.

Tidbit tray

Tidbit trays are found in two- and three-tier versions in both original and 1950s color variations. There are no official records of HLC making these as actual pieces, but there is evidence it made some of the original holed plates for construction of the trays. The trays that were drilled at the factory will have glaze inside the holes. Others with white holes were drilled and assembled post-factory (the hardware was and still is readily available).

Current suggested price $100-$200 (lower end for cobalt blue, light green, yellow, ivory and turquoise; higher end for red, forest green, chartreuse, rose, gray, and medium green)

Tidbit tray in ivory, light green, and cobalt blue.
$100-$200

Utility tray

Dimensions: 10-1/2" by 1-1/4"
Production Dates: 1936 to 1946.

This tray was a utilitarian piece as it could be used for a variety of functions: a base for the sugar and creamer or the salt and pepper set, or as a plate for pickles, olives, or celery. There are two slight variations to this tray. The original had a narrow, unglazed foot. The latter, introduced in 1938, had more slanted sides and a glazed foot (note a set of three pin marks equidistant from each other that form a triangle.) The latter version is typically marked "Genuine Fiesta/HLC USA." Production of red examples was halted in 1944.

Degree of Difficulty: 2

Cobalt Blue	**$49-$53**	Red	**$50-$55**
Ivory	**$45-$49**	Turquoise	**$48-$53**
Light Green	**$42-$47**	Yellow	**$44-$48**

Utility tray in light green. **$42-$47**

Utility tray in ivory. **$45-$49**

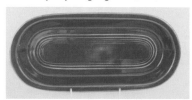
Utility tray in cobalt blue. **$49-$53**

Utility tray in turquoise. **$48-$53**

Utility tray in red. **$44-$48**

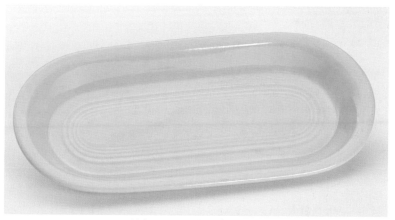

Utility tray in yellow. **$50-$55**

Tumblers

Juice tumbler

See Promotional Items.

Water tumbler

Dimensions: 4-1/2" by 3-3/8"
Production Dates: 1937 to 1946
The water tumbler differs from the juice tumbler in several ways. First and perhaps most obvious is the height—the water tumbler is approximately one inch taller. The water tumbler's sides flare more and have more pronounced, rounded rings. It can be marked either "Fiesta/HLC USA" or "Made in USA." Production of red examples was halted in 1944. There may be minute variations in height.

Degree of Difficulty: 1-2

Cobalt Blue	**$72-$80**
Ivory	**$70-$80**
Light Green	**$65-$68**
Red	**$75-$85**
Turquoise	**$65-$69**
Yellow	**$67-$70**

Three water tumblers in light green, **$65-$68,** cobalt blue, **$72-$80**, and turquoise, **$65-$69**.

Water tumblers in light green, **$65-$68,** yellow, **$67-$70**, and red, **$75-$85**.

Vases

Bud vase

Dimensions: 6-5/16" by 2-7/8"
Production Dates: 1936 to 1946
Made for slightly over 10 years, the bud vase seems to have sold well during its original run as is evident by how many are for resale today. Vintage pieces may be marked either "Fiesta/HLC USA" or "Made in USA." Production of red examples was halted in 1944. The bud vase is also part of the post-'86 line, with only a minute difference in height.

Degree of Difficulty: 1-2

Cobalt Blue	$100-$130
Ivory	$100-$120
Light Green	$85-$94
Red	$100-$130
Turquoise	$95-$115
Yellow	$85-$92

Bud vases in turquoise, **$95-$115,** cobalt blue, **$100-$130**, ivory, **$100-$120**, yellow, **$85-$92**, light green, **$85-$94**, and red, **$100-$130**.

Bud vase in cobalt blue. **$100-$130**

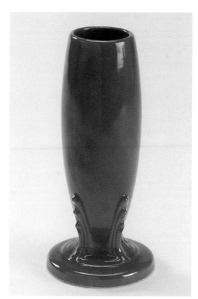

Bud vase in red. **$100-$130**

Grouping of vases in a variety of colors.

8" Vase

Dimensions: 7-15/16" by 4"
Production Dates: 1936 to 1946
The 8" vase was produced for approximately 10 years—four years longer than the 10" and 12" vases. Because red was discontinued in 1944, 8" vases in that color are slightly harder to find. The 8" vase may be marked "Made in USA." There are minute height variations in all three sizes.

Degree of Difficulty: 2-3

Cobalt Blue	**$725-$775**	Red	**$760-$800**
Ivory	**$740-$780**	Turquoise	**$600-$650**
Light Green	**$500-$590**	Yellow	**$540-$610**

8" vases in turquoise, **$600-$650,** red, **$760-$800,** and yellow, **$540-$610**.

8" vase in ivory. **$740-$780**

8" vase in yellow. **$540-$610**

10" Vase

Dimensions: 10" by 5-1/8"
Production Dates: 1936 to 1942
The 10" vase (like the 12" version) is marked "Fiesta HLC USA" in the mold. Light green and yellow are slightly less desirable than the other four colors. There are minute height variations in all three sizes.

Degree of Difficulty: 3

Cobalt Blue	$925-$990
Light Green	$810-$875
Ivory	$975-$1,000
Red	$1,000-$1,100
Turquoise	$900-$975
Yellow	$875-$900

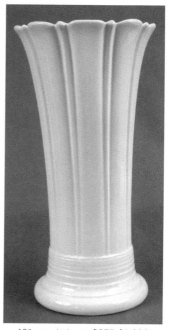

10" vase in ivory. **$975-$1,000**

Three vases—8", 10", and 12"—in red. **$760-$800, $1,000-$1,100,** and **$2,000-$2,100,** respectively

10" vase in
light green.
$810-$875

12" Vase

Dimensions: 11-3/4" by 5-15/16"
Production Dates: 1936 to 1942
One of the most expensive items in the line, the 12" vase is a centerpiece of any vintage Fiesta collection. Expect to pay $2,000 for one in red. Like the 10" vase, the 12" is typically marked "Fiesta/HLC USA." There are minute height variations in all three sizes.

Degree of Difficulty: 3

Cobalt Blue	**$1,300-$1,500**
Light Green	**$1,100-$1,200**
Ivory	**$1,150-$1,200**
Red	**$2,000-$2,100**
Turquoise	**$1,300-$1,450**
Yellow	**$1,100-$1,200**

12" vase in light green.
$1,100-$1,200

Left to right: 8", 10", and 12" vases in turquoise, yellow, and cobalt blue. **$600-$650, $875-$900,** and **$1,300-$1,500,** respectively

Promotional Items

For approximately four years, between 1939 and 1943, retailers were offered a series of special Fiesta pieces that could retail for $1. Some retailers took advantage of this promotion by selling them at a reduced price of 75 cents, while others sold them for upwards of $1.25. They were:

- Juice set—Yellow pitcher with six juice glasses, one in each of the six colors.

- Salad set—Yellow "unlisted" salad bowl with a red spoon and light green fork.

- French casserole—Yellow

- Sugar, creamer & tray set—Yellow sugar bowl and creamer on a cobalt blue tray

- Covered casserole with pie plate—Light green, red, and yellow

- Chop plate with metal handle

- Refrigerator set—Three bowls, one each in light green, cobalt blue, and yellow, and a lid in red.

Unlisted or promotional salad bowl

Dimensions: 9-3/4" by 3-1/2"
Production Dates: 1940 to 1943
Collectors have dubbed this bowl the "unlisted" salad bowl as it never appeared on any company price lists. They were sold along with a Kitchen Kraft fork and spoon, thus becoming the promotional salad set (see Kitchen Kraft). There are no interior rings on the bowls, and the impressed mark is "Fiesta/Made in USA/HLCo."

Degree of Difficulty: 2-3 for yellow, 5 for cobalt blue.

Cobalt Blue	$3,100-$3,300	Yellow	$100-$120

Unlisted salad bowl in yellow. **$100-$120**

Front: 11-3/4" fruit bowl in yellow with experimental spoon in turquoise. Back: Promotional salad bowl in cobalt blue, **$3,100-$3,300,** with experimental spoon in ivory.

Promotional salad bowl in cobalt blue, **$3,100-$3,300,** with red spoon and yellow fork. The promotional salad set that sold for approximately three years included a yellow bowl and a Kitchen Kraft spoon and fork.

Casserole with pie plate

Dimensions: Casserole–8-1/2", pie plate–9"
Production Dates: 1940 to 1943
A casserole and pie plate made up this $1 promotion. Most of the casserole bottoms are light green and the covers are red. This is how the sets were shipped from the factory–along with a 9" yellow pie plate. You could both bake and serve in the same piece, thus making it easy for the housewife of the early 1940s.

Degree of Difficulty: 2 for the pie plate, 3 for the casserole.

Light green and red casserole and yellow pie plate set: **$210-$235**

Promotional covered casserole with Fiesta red lid and Fiesta green bowl on a Fiesta yellow Kitchen Kraft 9" pie plate. This set in the same color combination also sold by Royal Metal Manufacturing. **$210-$235**

French Casserole

Dimensions: 11-3/4" by 4-1/4"
Production Dates: 1940 to 1943
The French casserole resembles a skillet with cover. You will also find its somewhat unusual stick handle repeated on the first creamer, the after dinner coffeepot, and the after dinner coffee cup (also called the demitasse cup). The French casserole is not easy to find, and often you will encounter either the top or bottom. If you come across a yellow lid, an easy way to tell if it is for the French casserole or the regular casserole is to check the underside. It if has a band of four rings, it is the regular casserole lid. Another way to determine which lid you have is to check the finial. The regular casserole has a finial that flares out more. Marked "Fiesta/Made in USA."

Degree of Difficulty: 4

Yellow	$275-$325

French casserole in yellow with yellow cover. **$275-$325**

French casserole with two additional standard covered casserole lids.

Various casserole lids. Center: Covered casserole lid in red; on either side are French casserole lids in yellow (standard) and light green (rare).

Creamer/sugar
and tray set

Dimensions:
Creamer (called "the individual"), 4-7/8" by 2-5/8" by 3-5/8"
Sugar Bowl (called "the individual"), 5-1/4" by 3-1/2" by 3-5/8"
Tray (figure-8), 10-3/8" by 5" by 7/8"
Production Dates: 1940 to 1943

The individual sugar and creamer, along with what collectors refer to as the figure-8 tray, were part of a promotional set. Notice the handles on the sugar and creamer: They are different from the other Fiesta sugar and creamer in that their handles are more of a "C" shape, rather than the round ring handle. They also tend to be lighter in weight.

The standard color combination was cobalt blue for the tray (stamped "Genuine Fiesta"), and yellow for the creamer and sugar (impressed "Made in USA"). But other colors, chiefly red and turquoise, have been found. Most cobalt blue trays will often show even the slightest surface scratching, as do all pieces in this glaze. Check sugar bowl lids for rim chips.

Degree of Difficulty: 3 for yellow sugar and creamer on cobalt blue tray; 4 for red creamer on turquoise tray; and 5 for anything else.

Red creamer	$325-$375
Cobalt Blue tray	$100-$150
Yellow creamer or sugar bowl	$90-$150 each
Turquoise tray	$450-$495

Promotional creamer and sugar in yellow, **$90-$150** each, with cobalt blue figure-8 tray, **$100-$150**.

Promotional creamer in red, **$325-$375,** on tray in turquoise, **$450-$495**—hard to find colors for these items.

Disk juice pitcher

Dimensions: 6" by 6-1/2" by 3-1/2"
Production Dates: 1939 to 1943
Most juice pitchers are yellow, as this was the color chosen for the promotion. Homer Laughlin Co. produced some in red for a special order. The difference in price between the yellow and red pitchers reflects the difficulty in obtaining one. During the 1939-1943 promotion, the juice pitcher, plus six tumblers, could be purchased for only $1. Usually marked "Fiesta/Made in USA."

Degree of Difficulty: 1 for yellow, 4 for red.

Red	$500-$580	Yellow	$55-$65

Juice set with disk juice pitcher in yellow, **$55-$65,** and six juice tumblers in Fiesta yellow, turquoise, red, cobalt blue, ivory, and green.

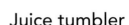
Juice tumbler

Dimensions: 3-1/2" by 2-1/2"

Production Dates: 1939 to 1943 (re-released in 1948 and again in 1951 in other colors)

Juice tumblers were made for special promotions in 1948 (called "Jubilee"), in about 1951 (for the Woolworth's "Rhythm" line that included Harlequin yellow), and as a promotion for Old Reliable Coffee. The tumblers were part of a seven-piece set that included the disk juice pitcher in gray (rare), red, turquoise (very rare), and both Fiesta and Harlequin yellow. There is a slight difference in the height and thickness of the juice tumbler. Seldom marked, they may have an "HLCo USA" stamp.

Degree of Difficulty: 1-2 for original colors, 3 for rose and gray, and 4 for forest green and chartreuse

Chartreuse	$800-$875	Light Green	$45-$48
Cobalt Blue	$50-$56	Red	$55-$60
Forest Green	$800-$850	Rose	$65-$75
Gray	$230-$250	Turquoise	$45-$48
Ivory	$50-$55	Yellow	$45-$48

Six Fiesta juice tumblers in yellow, turquoise, red, cobalt blue, ivory, and light green, plus a Fiesta juice tumbler in Harlequin rose.

Juice tumblers in chartreuse and Harlequin yellow, rose, and turquoise, with a red disk juice pitcher.

Notice the height difference between these juice tumblers in yellow and turquoise.

Notice the difference in the thickness of the sides of these juice tumblers in yellow and turquoise.

Juice tumbler in cobalt blue. **$50-$56**

Juice tumbler in yellow. **$45-$48**

Juice tumbler in red. **$55-$60**

Juice tumbler in light green. **$45-$48**

Juice tumbler in turquoise. **$45-$48**

Juice tumbler in ivory. **$50-$55**

POST '86
FIESTA
PIECES

Fiesta Returns

When Homer Laughlin reintroduced the updated Fiesta line on Feb. 28, 1986, a design that had been regarded as tired and outdated in the early 1970s was now seen as ripe with nostalgic appeal. Several Post-'86 items still use vintage mold shapes, including the two larger sizes of the disk pitchers, the sugar/creamer/tray set, the tripod and round candleholders, the C-handle creamer, the sauceboat, the 8" vase, and the salt and pepper shakers.

As with the vintage line, Homer Laughlin also licensed several companies to produce coordinating items for Post-'86 Fiesta, including cutlery, drawer pulls, glassware, kitchen timers, and even message boards.

Homer Laughlin continues to introduce new colors and items to the line, so check with local retailers.

Fiesta colors produced since 1986

Apricot—moderate, pale pinkish-orange (discontinued in 1998)

Black—(introduced in 1986)

Chartreuse—yellowish-green, more yellow than the original (produced from 1997 to 1999)

Cinnabar—burgundy or maroon (introduced in 2000)

Cobalt—dark navy (introduced in 1986)

Juniper—dark forest green (produced from 1999 to 2001)

Lilac—pastel purple or violet (produced from 1993 to 1995)

Peacock—bright bluish-green (introduced in 2005)

Pearl Gray—similar to vintage gray, more luminous (produced from 1999 to 2001)

Periwinkle Blue—grayish-blue (introduced in 1989)

Persimmon—dark orange-red (introduced in 1995)

Plum—deep purple (introduced in 2002)

Rose—bubblegum pink (produced from 1986 to 2005)

Sapphire—royal blue (sold only by Bloomingdale's in 1996 and 1997)

Scarlet—bright red (introduced in 2004)

Sea Mist Green—pastel, light green (produced from 1991 to 2005)

Shamrock—dark, grassy green (introduced in 2003)

Sunflower—bright, rich yellow (introduced in 2002)

Tangerine—bright orange (introduced in 2003)

Turquoise—greenish-blue (introduced in 1988)

White—(introduced in 1986)

Yellow—pale yellow (produced from 1987 to 2002)

Post-'86 items

Baker: Square, 9"

Bowls: Baker, 6" and 8" diameter; Bouillon, 6-3/4 ounce; Cereal, 10 ounce; Chili, 18 ounce; Chowder; Extra Large, 2 quarts; Fruit, 5-3/8" diameter; Gusto, 23 ounce; Large, 8-1/4" diameter; Medium, 6-7/8" diameter; Meow, 8 ounce; Mixing (7-1/2", 8-1/2" 9-1/2" diameters); Pasta, 12" diameter; Pedestal, 9-7/8" diameter; Rim Soup, 9" diameter; Small, 5-5/8" diameter; Vegetable (2-quart), 8-1/4" diameter; Vegetable (oval), 12-1/4" x 9".

Bread Tray: 12" by 5-3/4".

Candleholder: Round, 3-5/8" tall.

Cannisters: Small, 24 ounce; Medium, 52 ounce; Large, 80 ounce

Carafe with handle, 60 ounce.

Covered Butter, 7-1/8" long.

Covered Casserole, 70 ounce.

Covered sugar

Creamer

Cups: After Dinner ("AD"), 3 ounce; Jumbo, 18 ounce; Regular, 7-3/4 ounce.

Deep Dish Pie Baker: 10-1/4" diameter.

Disc Pitcher: Large, 67-1/4 ounce; Small, 28 ounce; Mini, 5 ounce.

Hostess Tray, 12-1/4" diameter.

Mugs: Café, 8 ounce; Cappucino, 21 ounce; Java, 12 ounce; Jumbo; Pedestal, 18 ounce; Regular, 10-1/4 ounce.

Oval Serving Dish, 12" by 9-1/8".

Planter/Saucer Set: 2 pieces, planter 3-5/8" x 6"; saucer 7" diameter.

Plates: Bread and butter, 6-1/8" diameter; Chop, 11-3/4" diameter; Commemorative; Dinner, 10-1/2" diameter; Luncheon, 9" diameter; Pizza, 15" diameter; Salad, 7-1/4" diameter; Snack with well, 10-1/2" diameter.

Platter: Egg, 13" diameter; Oval, 9-5/8" long; 11-5/8" long; 13-5/8" long; all-purpose, 15" diameter.

Ramekin: 4", 8 ounce.

Relish Tray, 9-1/2 ounce.

Salt & Pepper: Range set; Round set, each 2-1/5" by 2-5/8".

Sauceboat, 18-1/2 ounce.

Saucers: After Dinner ("AD"), 4-7/8" diameter; Jumbo, 6-3/4" diameter; Regular, 5-7/8" diameter.

Serving Tray: 13-1/2" x 6-1/4"

Snack Set: tray, 12" x 5-3/8"; cup, 3-1/8".

Spoon rest

Sugar and Creamer set: four pieces including figure-8 tray.

Sugar packet holder

Teapots: Covered, 44 ounce; Two-Cup.

Tool Crock

Trivet

Tumblers, 6-1/2 ounce.

Vases: Bud, 6" tall; Medium (called the 10"), 9-5/8" tall; Small, 8" tall; plus the Millennium I, II, and III; Monarch; Royalty.

Place setting with 10" plate, 7" plate and cup and saucer in lilac.

Three Post-'86 pitchers—disk water, disk juice and mini—in lilac.

Standard sugar bowl and Fiesta Mates 5-ounce creamer in black.

Fiesta advertising plate, 12" diameter chop, with mango red logo and type.

Millennium I vase in yellow.

Tripod candleholders in black and white.

Bread tray and cereal bowl in yellow.

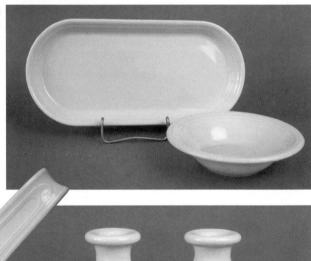

Spoon rest in sunflower.

Millennium candlesticks in yellow.

Bouillon cups in black and white.

Millennium III vase in persimmon.

Millennium II vase in turquoise.

Vases: two 8" in cinnabar (left) and turquoise, and a 10" in cobalt blue.

10" vase in lilac.

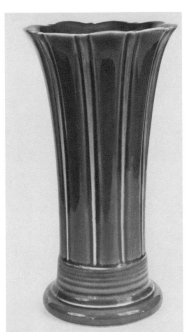

Carafe and four tumblers in chartreuse.

Napkin ring set in persimmon.

Commemorative presentation bowl sitting on an upside-down hostess bowl, both in persimmon, forming a large compote.

Hostess bowl in persimmon.

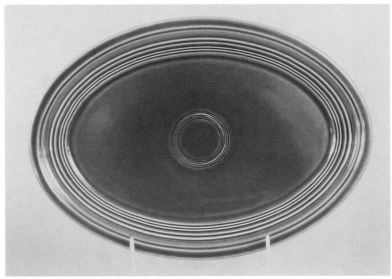

Large platter (13-1/2" wide) in cobalt blue.

Two smaller platters in turquoise and chartreuse.

Two sizes of pie bakers in persimmon and turquoise.

Range shakers in persimmon on a figure-8 tray.

Soup bowl in cobalt blue and cereal bowl in periwinkle.

Fruit bowl in chartreuse.

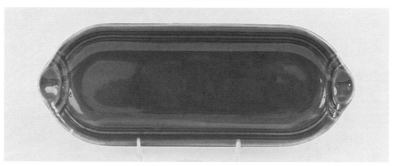

Relish or utility in cobalt blue.

Deep plates in turquoise and apricot.

Round serving tray in sapphire.

Tea server in black, and 2-cup teapot in persimmon (note difference in handles).

Two-cup teapot in chartreuse.

Trivets in cobalt and sunflower.

Sugar and creamer on figure-8 tray in turquoise.

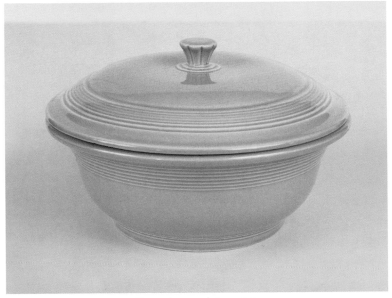

Covered casserole in apricot.

Salt and pepper shakers in chartreuse.

Sauceboat in lilac.

Covered butter dish in lilac.

Tom & Jerry mug in lilac.

Chop plate in lilac.

Soup bowl and cereal bowl in lilac.

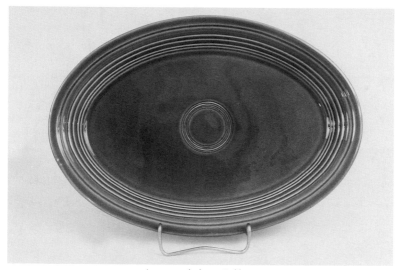

Large oval platter in lilac.

Pizza tray in persimmon with glaze flaw.

Hostess tray in turquoise.

Chili bowl in persimmon.

Jumbo mug and saucer
in turquoise.

Two-quart extra large bowl in pearl gray.

10" plate, cup and saucer, 7" plate and soup bowl in sapphire.

8-1/4" serving bowl in sapphire.

Round candleholders in black.

Cereal bowl and 7" plate in black.

Deep dish casserole in turquoise.

Bud vases in cinnabar, chartreuse, persimmon, turquoise, and black.

Bud vases in pearl gray, lilac, plum, juniper, and cobalt.

Bud vases in yellow, white, sea mist, apricot, and sunflower.

Tom & Jerry mugs in chartreuse, sunflower, shamrock, cinnabar, rose, sea mist, and plum. (One of these is also called the "Fan" or "Horizon" mug.)

Tom & Jerry mug in persimmon, 60th anniversary.

Tom & Jerry mugs in persimmon, white, pearl gray, lilac, juniper, and turquoise.

Tripod bowls in
chartreuse and juniper.

Disk water pitcher in
white with Mickey Mouse.

Goblet in white.

Warner Bros. pie baker in yellow.

Warner Bros. deep plate in rose.

Latte cups on persimmon and pearl gray.

Sugar packet holder in lilac.

Left, cappuccino mug in cinnabar; right, latte cup in pearl gray.

Goblet and fan mug in persimmon.

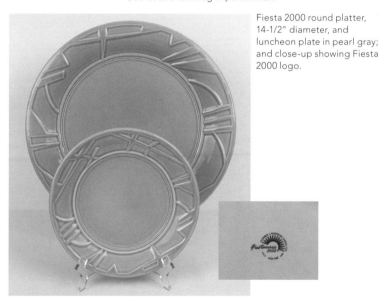

Fiesta 2000 round platter, 14-1/2" diameter, and luncheon plate in pearl gray; and close-up showing Fiesta 2000 logo.

Fiesta 2000 10" dinner plate in persimmon, and the all-purpose bowl in cobalt blue.

Bud vase in cobalt blue with floral decal, and a tumbler in black with the "Moon Over Miami" decal.

White disk juice pitcher with "Sun Porch" decal, and white tumbler with "Mexicana" decal.

White 9" plate with Millennium decal sold by Federated Department Stores.

Three sizes of mixing bowls in chartreuse (note color variation).

Three sizes of mixing bowls in juniper.

Medium bowl and ramekin in shamrock.

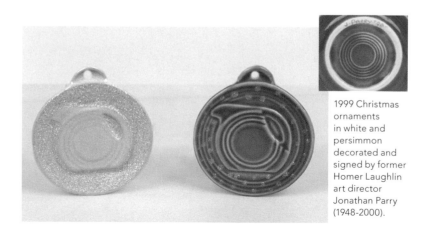

1999 Christmas ornaments in white and persimmon decorated and signed by former Homer Laughlin art director Jonathan Parry (1948-2000).

Original Post-'86 demitasse cup and saucer in yellow (redesigned in 2001), and mini disk pitcher in black with trial decal.

Child's set, including tumbler, bowl, and 9" plate with Noah's Ark decal.

Smiling face 9" plate in sunflower.

"My First Fiesta" set, including two-cup teapot in yellow, two ring-handle cups with saucers in periwinkle and rose, two 6" plates in yellow, and a creamer and covered sugar in turquoise; with original box.

Welled snack plate in juniper with a white bouillon cup.

Gusto bowl in sunflower.

Tool crocks in juniper and sunflower.

Pedestal bowl in cobalt blue.

Ramekins in apricot, shamrock, cobalt blue, and cinnabar.

Fiesta clock in chartreuse
(sold only for a matter of
months by JC Penney).

Amberstone, Casuals, Casualstone, Ironstone

None of the following four lines were intended to have Fiesta stamps, but since some styles and colors were shared, and production times overlapped, a few oddities exist. Some resources also combine the production dates for more than one line, but since each has distinct characteristics, we present them here as separate lines.

Amberstone

Amberstone dinnerwares—in both modified and original Fiesta shapes—were distributed as part of the Sheffield line by J&H International of Wilmette, Illinois, beginning in 1967 as a grocery store promotion. The rich, coffee-color glaze can be found on 27 items, from ashtrays to vegetable bowls, and also featured a stylized scroll and shield decoration in black, mostly on plates. Amberstone was produced for about two years.

Degree of Difficulty: 1

Fiesta Amberstone marmalade, left, and a Post-'86 standard sugar bowl in black.

Fiesta Amberstone covered butter dish.

Fiesta Amberstone coffee pot.

Fiesta Amberstone place setting with 10" plate, cup and saucer, and 6" bread plate.

Fiesta Amberstone deep plate.

Casuals

The Casuals line from the mid-1960s featured two patterns—"Yellow Carnation" and "Hawaiian 12-Point Daisy"—on plates that were matched with vintage-style yellow and turquoise pieces, respectively. The solid-color matching pieces included the ring-handle creamer, covered sugar, 5-1/2" fruit bowl, 8-1/2" nappy, and the teacup.

Degree of Difficulty: 2-3

Casualstone

The Casualstone line from 1970 was another short-lived grocery store promotion, distributed by Coventry Ware of Barberton, Ohio, and stamped "Coventry." It has the antique gold glaze and the plates have a stamped pattern of stylized leaves and scrolls. It was made in the same 27 shapes as Amberstone. Design changes include C-handles on the cups and creamer, and a more flared knob on the lids of covered pieces.

Degree of Difficulty: 1

Casualstone place setting with 10" plate, cup and saucer, and 7" plate in antique gold.

Casualstone 13" chop plate (front and back) in antique gold.

Ironstone

Fiesta Ironstone was introduced in 1969 with the colors of antique gold, mango red (same as original red), and turf green (olive). The new shapes included a 5-1/2" fruit/dessert bowl, a 6-1/2" soup/cereal bowl, a 10-1/2" salad bowl, an 8-7/8" vegetable bowl, a covered casserole (like several other Ironstone pieces, available only in antique gold), a straight-side coffee mug, a sauceboat underplate or "stand," and a covered sugar bowl without handles. Other pieces based on vintage shapes also received restyled knobs and handles, and these design updates can also be found in Amberstone and Casualstone.

Degree of Difficulty: 2-3

Cup and saucer in turf green.

Cup and saucer in antique gold.

Amberstone brown fruit/dessert bowl, and two Ironstone fruit/dessert bowls in turf green and antique gold.

Ironstone soup/cereal bowl in mango red.

Ironstone sauceboat stands in antique gold, turf green, and mango red.

Ironstone 7" plate in turf green.

Ironstone 7" plate in antique gold.

Ironstone 10" plate in antique gold.

Ironstone 10" plate in turf green.

Ironstone salt and pepper shakers in antique gold and Amberstone brown.

Ironstone sauceboat in turf green.

Ironstone oval platter in turf green.

Ironstone covered sugar in antique gold, and a creamer in antique gold in original
packaging and with store coupon, next to a covered sugar in Amberstone.

Ironstone saucers in antique gold and turf green in original packaging.

Ironstone cups in antique gold, in original packaging.

Ironstone 7" plate, and cups in original packaging, all in turf green.

Striped Fiesta

Fiesta pieces with stripes came in two styles: the first came near the beginning of production in the late 1930s, and has three concentric rings—in blue and red—around the edges of ivory pieces that include bowls, casseroles, cups, lids, plates, and saucers. The other style is part of a cake set numbering five or seven pieces sold by Sears during the mid-1940s, and features two bands of color, usually green or maroon, on ivory and yellow 10" and 7" plates. These pieces are usually valued at three to four times the price of similar examples without stripes.

Saucer and 7" plate with three blue stripes.

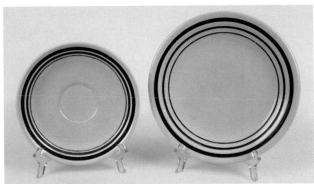

6" plate and 5 1/2" fruit bowl with red stripes.

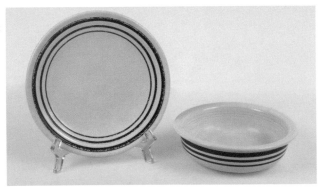

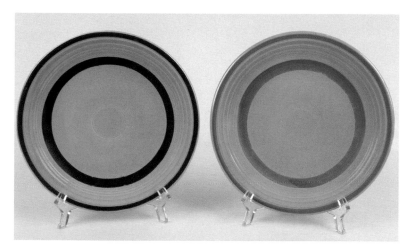

Striped plates sold as part of cake sets by Sears, circa 1937: 7" plates in green on yellow and maroon on yellow; 10" and 7" plates in green on ivory.

Fiesta Kitchen Kraft

Items in the Fiesta Kitchen Kraft line were produced from 1938 to the mid-1940s, in cobalt blue, light green, red, and yellow, and included 21 pieces. An impressed mark, "Fiesta Kitchen Kraft U.S.A.," and an applied label, "Guaranteed Fiesta Kitchen Kraft U-S-A," were both used. Kitchen Kraft shapes in Fiesta colors were also offered in special promotions for the Royal Metal Manufacturing Co. of Chicago, and in combination with regular Fiesta pieces. Some items are not difficult to find, but those with original labels bring a premium.

Fiesta Kitchen Kraft individual casserole in light green.
$150-$160

Fiesta Kitchen Kraft cake lifter in yellow. **$140-$150**

Fiesta Kitchen Kraft cake lifter in light green. **$140-$150**

Fiesta Kitchen Kraft cake lifter in cobalt blue, **$150-$160,** shown with salad fork.

Fiesta Kitchen
Kraft shakers
in light green
and cobalt blue.
$90-$110

Fiesta Kitchen
Kraft shakers
in red.
$90-$110/pair

Fiesta Kitchen Kraft refrigerator sets, with three bodies in light green, cobalt blue, and
ivory, **$45-$55 each**, and two covers in cobalt blue and red, **$75-$85 each**.

Royal Metal pie plate in Fiesta red with metal stand. **$60-$70/pair**

Fiesta Kitchen Kraft salad fork in light green. **$125-$140**

Fiesta Kitchen Kraft cake plate in yellow. **$50-$60**

Two Fiesta Kitchen Kraft covered jars, medium (7 in. diameter), **$250-$300,** and large (8 in. diameter) in light green, **$300-$350**, the smaller with original label.

Fiesta Kitchen Kraft medium covered jar in yellow. **$250-$300**

Fiesta Kitchen Kraft cake plate in cobalt blue. **$60-$70**

Fiesta Kitchen Kraft covered casserole in light green. **$80-$110**

Fiesta Kitchen Kraft individual casseroles in light green and yellow. **$150-$160** each

Fiesta Kitchen Kraft salad spoon in red. **$140-$150**

Fiesta Kitchen Kraft salad spoon in light green. **$125-$140**

Kitchen Kraft covered casserole in cobalt blue on a Royal Chrome stand. **$130-$140/pair**

Pie plate in blue, part of the Zephyr line made by Cronin China Co., Minerva, Ohio, in the 1930s.

Kitchen Kraft 9-1/2" pie plate in Fiesta yellow, left, and 9-1/2" yellow pie plate, part of the Zephyr line made by Cronin China Co., Minerva, Ohio, in the 1930s. (Note difference in rim width.)

9-1/2" pie plates in colors similar to light green and cobalt blue, but actually part of the Zephyr line made by Cronin China Co., Minerva, Ohio, in the 1930s.

Fiesta Kitchen Kraft salad fork in yellow with original paper label.

Fiesta Kitchen Kraft salad spoon in red, never-produced spoon in ivory (rare), never-produced spoon in turquoise (rare), and salad fork in yellow.

Commemoratives & Souvenirs

As with any group of collecting enthusiasts, the Homer Laughlin China Collectors Association holds annual conferences and issues commemorative pieces to mark the occasions. Formed in 1998 as an all-volunteer, member-operated organization, HLCCA is dedicated to providing education and communication for all those interested in the wares of the Homer Laughlin China Co., from 1873 to the present. *The Dish*, the official publication of HLCCA, is published quarterly.

Homer Laughlin
China Collector's
Association disk
juice pitchers: The
1930 Chrysler Building
pitcher was issued in
1999; the 1931 Dick Tracy
pitcher was issued in
2000; the 1932 radio
pitcher was also issued
in 2000; 1933 zeppelin
motif was issued in 2001;
the 1934 ship design was
issued in 2002.

White tool crock and small pie baker with Homer Laughlin China Collector's Association 2002 Conference decals.

Two mugs with the Ms. Bea decal, from 1999 and 2000; commemorative plate from the 2001 HLCCA conference.

Presentation bowl in cobalt blue, gilded for use as the HLCCA exhibition Grand Award and bearing a facsimile of Jonathan Parry's signature, presented to Fred Mutchler.

Disk water pitchers in cobalt blue, presented as HLCCA awards to Fred Mutchler in 1999 and 2000, each with a facsimile of the signature of Frederick H. Rhead, original designer of the Fiesta line.

Homer Laughlin Fiesta souvenir plate, 6-1/4" diameter.

Top and bottom of presentation bowl (in persimmon) marking the 500,000,000th piece of Fiesta.

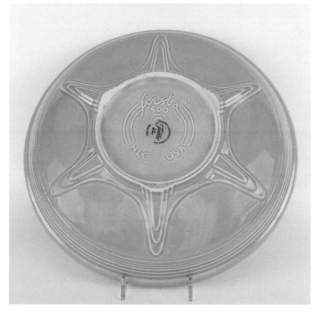

Top and bottom of presentation bowl (in chartreuse) marking the 500,000,000th piece of Fiesta.

Left, 2002 HLCCA Gold Award in a disk water pitcher in cobalt blue; right, 2001 HLCCA Silver Award in a Fiesta disk juice pitcher in pearl gray.

Fiesta 60th anniversary beverage set: disk water pitcher and four tumblers in lilac, all with the anniversary mark.

Fiesta Club of America hostess tray in chartreuse, from 1998. (This group was active for about five years—1995 to 1999—and issued decal trays annually. The first, in lilac, is valued at about **$300-$350.)**

50th anniversary (1986) ring-handle mugs, 3-1/4" tall, in white, each having the anniversary sticker.

Fiesta 60th anniversary beverage set: disk water pitcher and four tumblers in sapphire, all with the anniversary mark, sold by Bloomingdale's.

Fiesta Go-Alongs

The term "go-alongs" refers to items made to coordinate with Fiesta colors. We present a sampling of vintage items here. Examples include flatware, glasses, metal holders, and accessories, even linens and kitchen storage pieces like breadboxes and trash cans.

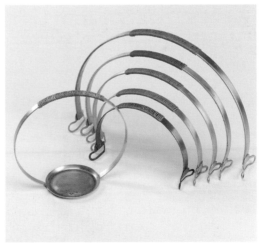

Raffia-wrapped metal handles were Fiesta go-alongs.

Four individual salt and pepper shakers and a "coaster" ashtray, which came with a circa 1941 "All Fiesta Ensemble."

Go-along glassware with Mexican motifs referred to as the cactus, pot, and sombrero.
$15-$20 each

Go-along glassware with banded tops. **$10-$15** each

Go-along glassware from the original four-place ensemble in 1939, also called "the dancing lady" ensemble because it includes the only appearance on glass of the Fiesta dancing lady. Rare. **$60-$70** each

A collection of go-along utensils made by Sta-Brite Corp., New Haven, Connecticut, with color-matched handles; the blue handles often turn a purple-black hue.

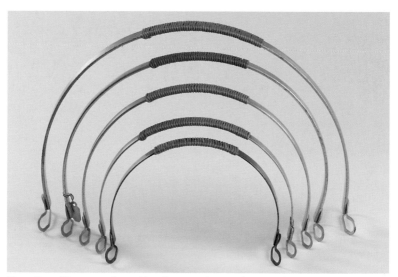

These five raffia-wrapped metal handles were designed to go with Fiesta plates. The smallest handle fits a 7" plate, the next size fits a 9" plate, the middle size fits a 10" plate (as well as a relish tray), the second largest size fits a 13" chop plate, and the largest size fits a 15" chop plate.

This raffia-wrapped metal handle fits a #2 mixing bowl, turning it into an ice bucket.

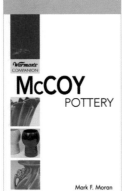